An Uncomm[...]

FitzRoy and Holkham 1808-1837

Mary-Anne Garry

Larks Press

Published by the Larks Press,
Ordnance Farm House, Guist Bottom, Dereham NR20 5PF
01328 829207

Printed by the Lanceni Press, Fakenham

British Library Cataloguing-in-Publication Data
A catalogue record for this book is available
from the British Library.

With grateful thanks to the Earl of Leicester of Holkham Hall
and Christine Hiskey, the archivist there, for allowing me access to
the estate documents.

ISBN 0 948400 46 3

For R.V.

Baron Southampton, FitzRoy's father, by Sir Joshua Reynolds
(The Royal Collection, Copyright Her Majesty the Queen)

An Uncommon Tenant,
FitzRoy and Holkham 1808 - 1837

When in 1808 Lt.Colonel the Honourable William FitzRoy, late of the Coldstream Guards and on half pay from the 85th Regiment of Foot, became the tenant at Kempstone Lodge Farm (nr. Litcham in Norfolk) one of the many farms on Thomas William Coke's great estate of Holkham, his background and upbringing marked him out as being quite different from the average member of the tenantry. In his own words he explained: "I was not to be considered in the light of a common Tenant, indeed I would not have taken the place under such circumstances" [Holkham Letter Book: 9th February 1817, FitzRoy to Blaikie]. In fact he was more than a mere exception; as an aristocrat he was unique.

Typical tenants of the period often came from part of the Holkham 'family', the brother, son or cousin of an existing tenant, and while they were chosen for intelligence and diligence, they were to be first and foremost able farmers. The general custom of the Holkham Estate was to grant 21 year leases and, depending on the 'wealth' the incoming tenant bought with him, and which they were prepared to invest, certain improvements were made to the farm houses and premises, the cost to be shared with the landlord. Thus when Mr Turner, who styled himself 'Gent' and farmed at Castle Acre, enlarged his house and installed marble chimney-pieces, he paid his half share and billed Holkham for the balance. It was not unusual for these joint investments to come to many hundreds of pounds. At Kempstone FitzRoy enjoyed the same arrangement: Holkham agreed to pay £300 for a new cottage to be built and a further £676 towards other alterations. But the majority of the improvements FitzRoy paid for himself, and he spent the huge amount of £6,000; had it been for sale, the whole farm of 400 acres would not have cost more to buy freehold. He began with the highest ideals and he wished to learn all he could of farming from Coke: "I had set my heart on making Kempstone perfect" he wrote in December 1816. To attempt an understanding of why FitzRoy, albeit in an age when renting was far more common than it is today, spent this enormous sum of money on a place that was not his own, and never would be, and of how and why Coke agreed to it, it is necessary to examine something of the world from which he came.

William FitzRoy was born into an aristocratic family, the son of a Baron and the nephew of a Duke. His father, the younger brother of the 3rd Duke of Grafton, was a soldier and MP, who in 1780 was created Baron Southampton. His mother was Anne, daughter and co-heir of Admiral Sir Peter Warren. The Southampton/FitzRoys married in 1758 and had a large family, 15 children, of whom 11 reached adulthood. This was thought a desirably large number of offspring and the progeny was commented on in the London newspapers, in August 1780 following an announcement of Her Majesty's lying in at Windsor, the Editor adds: "General FitzRoy, the Archbishop of York and his Majesty each have thirteen [living] children." [*Norfolk Chronicle* 19 August 1780.] William was born in 1773, the 7th son, and 13th child: two days after his birth Horace Walpole wrote to Lady Ossory "Mrs FitzRoy has got a seventh boy. Between her and the Queen London will be like the Senate of Rome, an assembly of princes." [*Walpole's Correspondence*, Ed.W.S.Lewis Vol.32, a reference to their royal origins as descendants of Charles II].

The Southampton/FitzRoys' chief residence was in Highgate. General FitzRoy inherited the estate of Totenhall Manor, (the site of the house in Tottenham Court Road, on the edge of Fitzrovia) which comprised parts of Camden Town, Kentish Town and Highgate and purchased land in Chalk Farm and land in Ireland. [settlement made 13 July 1790, doc.HA/513/4/45 Bury Records Office].The estate had been leased to his great-grandmother, Isabella, Countess of Arlington in her own right for three lives, she being the wife of the 1st Duke of Grafton. The second Duke obtained a fresh lease in 1723, which was terminated by an Act of Parliament in 1768 when the freehold was sold by the canons of St Paul's Cathedral to General FitzRoy for a ground rent of £300 per annum. The freehold land covered 25 acres. [*London County Council Survey of London, Highgate* Vol.XVII 1936]. (The estate included a FitzRoy Chapel in St Pancras, where in 1803 Sydney Smith was appointed alternate morning preacher at £50 p.a. [Peter Virgin, *Sydney Smith,* Harper Collins 1994].)

A casual glance at the modern map shows the high proportion of FitzRoy associated names in that part of London; Warren Street, after his wife's family, is one of the less obvious. As well as a developer, Southampton/FitzRoy was also a benefactor, in 1790 he founded St Pancras Female Charity School. [F.E.Hansford, *Story of the Little Georgian House*] His portrait by Sir Joshua Reynolds is in the Queen's collection at Buckingham Palace.

At the northernmost point of his property, on the western slope of Highgate, with views to Kenwood, where today the road is marked FitzRoy Park, the General took over a small farm of 100 acres, the site of an old farmhouse called Sherricks. Highgate, high above London, looked down on the expanding city which at this time was surrounded for the greater part by a chain of brick kilns, steaming and smoking, refuse heaps, stagnant pools and undrained marsh land. Then as now Hampstead and Highgate, with their green and pleasant fields intersected by the river Fleet and its tributaries were somewhat of an oasis.

A few years later, in 1787, on her move to Hampstead, Mrs Barbauld, who had East Anglian connections, wrote a description of the farm in a letter to her brother John Aiken:

"...... Hampstead and Highgate are mutually objects to each other, and the road between them is delightfully pleasant, lying along Lord Mansfield's fine woods, and the Earl [sic] of Southampton's ferme ornée, Lady Mansfield and Lady Southampton, I am told, are both admirable dairy women, and so jealous of each other's fame that they have had many heart-burnings, and have once or twice been very near a serious falling out on the dispute: which of them could make the greatest quantity of butter from such a number of cows. On observing the beautiful smoothness of the turf in some of the fields about this place, I was told the gentlemen to whom they belong had them rolled like a garden plot..." [Betsy Rodgers, *Georgian Chronicle, Mrs Barbauld and Her Family*, Methuen 1958]

Philip Southcote is generally credited with being the inventor of the 'ferme ornée' or ornamental farm, (despite its name a thoroughly English concept though imitated by the French). In 1735 he bought the 150 acre Woburn farm in the Thames Valley, and planted 35 acres with trees and shrubs through which wound an ornamental walk. More shrubs merged with the native hedgerows dividing the fields, for this was a working farm; the dairy, haystacks, pastures and tillage being every bit as important as the ruined Chapel, Gothic buildings, seats, alcoves and bridges. Unlike his contemporary, Kent, who sought to create an Elysium, suggesting a place of almost otherwordliness, Southcote's ambition was an Arcady, a picturesque but remunerative landscape, the countryside as it could and should be, combining beauty with produce, an idyll of milk maids and shepherdesses. The eighteenth century was the age of reason, which conversely produced a sophisticated longing for an escape into the unreal. In the 1760s Tahiti was discovered and the idea of the Noble Savage living in innocent simplicity and happiness led Diderot the French philospher and friend of Rousseau, among many others, into an intense romantic enthusiasm which was highly infectious. In England Hawkesworth's account (second hand) of Captain Cooke's South Sea journals had the same effect. [Alan Moorehead, *The Fatal Impact*, Hamish Hamilton 1966]. Kent may be said to have reflected these ideas, the art of escape, but Southcote and his ornamental farm, while including the ideals of classical mythology, combined the realistic with the aesthetic and never allowed that slip into the dreamworld.

One of the few remaining, and probably the best known example of a ferme ornée is that made for Marie-Antoinette at Versailles. In contrast to the formality of the existing gardens there, created by Le Notre, (André le Notre 1613-?) garden designer to King Louis XIV, the Sun King, who took the components of the Renaissance garden and with French logic created a huge vista of geometrical shapes, a large proportion of which was covered by either water or wood, Marie-Antoinette had the acres given to her by her husband (Louis XVI) laid out in le style anglais and at le Hameau, the little farmhouse designed by Hubert Robert in 1774, played at farming. It was the age of Boucher and Fragonard. Le style anglais was accepted as a softer gentler garden with no harsh lines, nature helped, not schooled. [Miles Hadfield: *A History of British Gardening*, Hutchinson and Co. 1960.]

The fashion for these farms continued into the nineteenth century, in particular the vogue for butter making. In 1802 at Holkham the youngest daughter of Thomas William Coke was aged seven; with her sisters married and her mother lately dead, Miss Coke was paid

4

Lord Southampton's Lodge at Highgate, after the remodelling in the 1790s, published by Robert Sayer, 1792

between £6 and £11 a month for "supplying cream and butter to the Mansion", an arrangement that lasted until she was seventeen. [Holkham Account Book A/48 to A/49]. And the custom was still practised in the early years of this century when at Sandringham Queen Alexandra and her daughters made butter in a dairy decorated with Minton tiles, (now sadly demolished).

But in the 1790s the FitzRoy farmhouse was remodelled, and Repton was employed to improve the park. A print published by Robert Sayer in 1792 of "Lord Southampton's Lodge at Highgate" shows a classical house with central portico, a sweeping driveway and a park with only a few sheep in the foreground. Besides the farm, the Southampton/FitzRoys owned a town house in Upper Brook Street, Mayfair, and in common with the fashion of the times they spent part of the year (generally August and September) travelling. The Duke of Grafton had a seat at Euston in Suffolk and another in Northamptonshire, and these two houses were much visited by all the FitzRoys, and there was no shortage of them; the Duke also had a large family, with sixteen children from two marriages.

Several accounts of the Southampton/FitzRoys are to be found in the *Journals of Lady Mary Coke*, which were written as letters between 1766 and 1774. The widow of Thomas Coke's heir, Edward, Lady Mary Coke survived her husband, who died in 1753, for 58 years. Much of her time was spent in London. She records in August 1766 (her journal was written before General FitzRoy père was created Baron Southampton) calling on Mrs FitzRoy: "They and Miss Lloyd were to have set out for Paris on Saturday but Col. FitzRoy was taken ill with a sore throat and fever." On the following page "Before ten o'clock dress'd, breakfasted and wrote a note to Mrs FitzRoy with the lace man's directions at Paris." The FitzRoys went to Paris several times, sometimes taking their children with them, and were almost certainly presented at Court. In London they and Lady Mary Coke often dined with the French Ambassador (le Comte de Guerchy). Their travelling companion, Miss Lloyd, appears to have been a housekeeper at Kensington Palace, someone much admired by Horace Walpole, but described by Lady Mary as "a Concierge, an Office so low in France she could not be received at the Palais Royal." [*The Journal of Lady Mary Coke* Vol.2].

It is clear that the FitzRoys moved in the best circles of society, and from the *Journal* it is evident that Mrs FitzRoy's constant pregnancies did not deter her from enjoying masquerades, suppers following visits to the Opera, and the never ending fascination of Loo, a card game to which most of Lady Mary Coke's friends were addicted. In 1768 Mrs FitzRoy won 50gns in an evening. They frequently met at the house of Princess Amelia, the favourite daughter of George II, who with Lady Hertford (née FitzRoy their aunt), formed the pivot of their circle. Unlimited loo and strong language were to Princess Amelia's taste [Roger Fulford: *George the Fourth*, Duckworth 1935] Lady Mary provides an example: "Mr and Mrs FitzRoy came so late the Princess sat down to play before they arrived, and Mr FitzRoy, having dined at a Tavern, was in rather too great spirits." [*The Journal of Lady Mary Coke*, Vol.3.] On another evening at the Princess's, Lady Mary Coke records "Mrs FitzRoy behaved in the most indecent manner I ever saw." The following day Princess Amelia apologized to Lady Mary on Mrs FitzRoy's behalf for the unkindness shown, and at a further meeting the Princess referred to Mrs FitzRoy's behaviour, stopping only at the arrival of the guilty party. [Ibid.Vol.3.] The relationship continued to be strained, though Lady Mary made an effort to restore harmony: "I behaved the same and was as easy with her as I was before She used me so ill at Princess Amelia's." [Ibid.Vol.3]

It was in her interest to remain on good terms, for Mrs FitzRoy supplied her with news (gossip), but occasionally she was let down, such as at the time of the Duke of Grafton's re-marriage after his divorce in 1769, when the FitzRoys proved to be uncharacteristically silent: "They were so secret that day they said not a word of it." [Ibid. Vol.3] And from here on her feelings towards the FitzRoys cooled.

In 1770 Lady Mary records "Lord Molyneux was driving in a machine, the name of which I don't know, his lady, Mrs FitzRoy and two others, and overturned them down a precipice. Mrs FitzRoy, six months gone with child, jumped out." And in the following year "Mrs FitzRoy is returned to England, again with Child and does not look in beauty." This was her eleventh pregnancy. But the parties and gaming went on. In June 1773 the FitzRoys held a large fête and Horace Walpole wrote that he drank tea "with all the fashionable world at Mr

FitzRoy's Farm on Thursday, blown there by the north wind."
[*Walpole's Correspondence, to Lady Ossory*, OUP]. Lady Mary had
been invited, but declined to go. [*The Journal of Lady Mary Coke*,
Vol.4]. In August 1774 she says the FitzRoys and children are "gone
to Paris." [Ibid, Vol.4]. A month or so later they are returned, "Lord
March, Lord Frederick Cavendish, Mr Selwyn and Mr and Mrs Fitz-
Roy dined at Lord Hertford's. The FitzRoys made us all wait till after
five O'Clock: they were three weeks in Paris and Mrs FitzRoy is so
charmed with every thing She saw, that She can talk of nothing else:
She asked Lord Hertford and I, if we did not think it much prettier to
hang a room in part and as they do in Paris, and as they formerly did
in England - which I believe She did not know - for nothing but what
is done in France can please her. Such as her, I agree with Lord John
Cavendish, shou'd not be allow'd to go out of their own Country; 'tis
a sort of Affectation that is terrible." [Ibid, Vol 4]. 1774 is the last
year of the published Journal, and in the same year General FitzRoy
became MP for Thetford. He died in 1797, and his wife in 1807; they
are buried in St James's Church, Hampstead Road.

***

Such was the glittering world in which William FitzRoy grew up. His
five older brothers appear on the Eton register, the younger ones
leaving at the age of 11, but William's name is not there. Charles
Bosanquet (1769 - 1850) records, in an unpublished manuscript of
autobiographical notes, that several FitzRoy children, both Graftons
and Southamptons, (among other children from "many families of
distinction"), were his contemporaries at Newcome's Academy in
Hackney. This school is described as a "curiously mixed, fashionable,
semi-barbarous seminary for the sons of noblemen and gentlemen,
with a curriculam, if haphazard and scrappy, rooted in high tradition.
The three R's subordinated to classic drama." Military victories and
political events were exploited in the cause of education and
celebrated with whole holidays. The conditions were spartan, small
boys were often sent out on cold November evenings to pilfer turnips
from neighbouring fields. The school took boys of six or seven and
kept those who could survive its rigours until they were

sixteen. Not surprisingly the academic standard was extremely low. Another of the Academy's old boys who wrote his impressions of the place in later years was Stratford Canning: "How the Muses ever came to settle at Hackney under the auspices of Mr Richard Newcome I find it difficult to conceive." [*Lives and Letters, Thomas Creevey's Papers 1793-1838*, edited by John Gore, Penguin 1985].

It is certainly true that William did feel his education had been wanting; in one of his letters to Blaikie at Holkham he laments, "I wish I had your art of writing......it is not a word too little, not a word too much." [Holkham Letter 16.]

In 1790, at the age of 17 and following the family tradition, he joined the Army, the first Battalion of the Coldstream Guards, as an Ensign. The British Army had been much depleted since the American Wars of Independence in the 1770s, and was at this time, with the exception of the the Guards regiments, ill disciplined and inefficient. The fault was Pitt's who throughout his ten year administration stuck to a policy of avoiding war, and subsequently of failing to maintain the army. However, in 1793 he was forced to re-consider. The French were uncomfortably close by, threatening to invade Holland, where the state of the Dutch army was even worse than the British, for not only were they badly trained but they had very little equipment. As a defensive measure it was decided to send several battalions of the Guards to Holland, not to fight, but to stand as a sort of buffer discouraging the enemy from embarking on an invasion of England. Their arrival had, not surprisingly, a disquieting effect upon the French troops and before long, under their Colonel, Frederick Duke of York (he of the Nursery Rhyme), the first Battalion of the Coldstream Guards was engaged in active service. One of their first battles was fought at Nivelle, in what is now Belgium, in a wood on 8th May 1793 when 70 men killed or wounded. FitzRoy's immediate commanding officer was Lt. Colonel Thomas Bosville.

The whole campaign, which spread along the coast of the Low Countries, that is into Belgium and northern France, lasted from 1793 to 1795 and was generally agreed to have been disastrous for the British. Not only was the army too small, (6,000 men), and the new recruits in the main either old men or weak boys, but the conditions were appalling. Severe weather was partly to blame, but the supplies were appalling. Severe weather was partly to blame, but the supplies needed to support the troops were hopelessly inadequate and even the normally well organized Guardsmen found themselves with no shelter and few rations. "Forty English Guardsmen huddled round a plundered waggon." [J.W.Fortescue, *History of the British Army*]. FitzRoy's elder brother, George, later 2nd Lord Southampton, was also engaged in this campaign, as was his younger brother Robert and their cousin General Lord Charles FitzRoy. A flavour of the ill-fated débâcle is recorded in letters written by Lord Charles FitzRoy to his father, the Duke of Grafton, e.g. "From a camp near Menin 25th September 1793: We were obliged to retire from our situation before Dunkirk for by this time the lowness and stinking water of the country must have made more havoc among the troops than even a formidable Garrison open to constant reinforcements could have done." [HA 513/4/96 - 107 Bury R.O.]. Illness was rife and there were two more years to be endured. The expedition, although successful in its objective of preventing the French invading England, thanks largely to Britain's allies, ended disgracefully in 1795. Blame was heaped upon the Duke of York who was immortalized in verse - though Holland is a bit short on hills and he was not old, but 28. However his leadership was certainly at fault and he was not helped by incompetent politicians. By November 1794 11,000 soldiers out of the 21,000 in British pay in Flanders had died of disease and neglect.

[During this time it is possible that FitzRoy visited Lady Bedingfield in Ghent, see below p.68/69; references to various members of the FitzRoy family who stayed with her during the many years she lived there are recorded in the *Jerningham Letters*.]

***

In 1795 FitzRoy was made a Captain, and for the next five years saw no more active service until 1801, when the Coldstream Guards were sent to Egypt. Here, as part of General Abercrombie's force, they fought a successful campaign against the French (under General Kleber) for the possession of Alexandria. The *Norwich Mercury* records the names of every causalty. Ten officers were killed and sixty wounded, FitzRoy's name does not appear; it would seem he came through this campaign unscathed. General Abercrombie was not so fortunate, his name heads the fatalities, with a Lt. Warren of the Guards, son of Admiral Warren, most probably FitzRoy's cousin.

By January 1st 1802 the Guards were back in Colchester Barracks, and later that year FitzRoy became a Lt. Colonel. [*Norwich Mercury* 1801/2].

In peacetime, or in between wars, officers in the Coldstream Guards, nicknamed 'The Gentlemen's Sons', enjoyed a high standard of living. They came from the higher echelons of society and needed considerable private means to pay not only for the service dress, the normal wear, but also for elaborate state uniforms worn to the various functions held at Windsor or St James's. There were large mess bills to meet (the Guards officers dined in lavish fashion), and various other costs such as the desirability of belonging to one of the London clubs, Whites or Brookes. J.W.Fortescue recorded that the Officers of the Guards were able to command more respect from their men as a result of their upbringing and he regretted the fact that more aristocratic families did not send their sons into the Army. The Nulli Secundus Club for members and ex-members of the Coldstream Guards was founded in 1783, William FitzRoy and his elder brother George both joined in 1794. In 1883 when the Club held its first centenary celebration dinner, the then presiding Lt.Colonel of the Regiment was Colonel G.R.FitzRoy. [Lt.Col.Ross of Bladenburg C.B., *A History of the Coldstream Guards from 1815 to 1895*, London 1896.]

Of William's many brothers and sisters, two of his brothers became Generals, as he did, while his sisters married Generals, or failing that, Lords. His elder brother, Henry, who died at 30, had married the Duke of Wellington's sister, Anne. In London, a generation on, his family continued to play a prominent part in society, the next Lady Hertford (FitzRoy's first cousin) was intimate with the Prince Regent, to the extent she was known as his Empress, and the Prince Regent's sister, another Princess Amelia, was deeply in love with General Charles FitzRoy, William's elder brother. [Roger Fulford, *George the Fourth*, Duckworth 1935]

***

William FitzRoy (hereinafter to be called FitzRoy only) married in 1799. His wife was Catherine Haughton daughter and heir of Sir Simon Clarke Bt. of Jamaica. (This marriage must have pleased his mother, now a widow, for she was intensely ambitious for all her children after her eldest son .married a beautiful but dowerless girl, Laura Keppel.)

The following year, FitzRoy, still in the army, rented a country house or shooting estate at Fornham All Saints near Bury St Edmunds, Suffolk, his landlords were the guardians of Thomas Gage, then a minor. [*Bury and Norwich Post*, September 1800. Game Duty list.]

[*NOTE*: The Game Duty lists were published each year in the local paper, in 1800 the General Certificate cost 3 gns, and was needed for the right to shoot over Manor land. Gamekeepers Certificates were also required, they cost lgn. and lists of gamekeepers, one for each Manor, were also published in the papers. In the case of Holkham where several adjacent Manors were owned by one person, (Coke), one or two gamekeepers only are named. Coke held the shooting rights over all the farms/Manors on his Estate, so that no tenant's name ever appears on these lists, though the rights were sometimes hired out to the tenants, with the exception of FitzRoy. For example: in September 1810 The Hon.Wm.FitzRoy obtained the Game Duty Certificate for Kempstone, nevertheless Coke appointed the Kempstone gamekeeper, William Ransome, a Holkham man. [*Norfolk Chronicle*, 13th September 1810.].

In December 1802, a year after his return from Egypt, FitzRoy's first child was born a son, William Simon Haughton Clarke. And from that year to 1807 inclusive, FitzRoy appears in the annual Game Duty Lists published in the *Norfolk Chronicle* and *Norwich Gazette* paying the required 3 gns. for Great Witchingham, Norfolk.

The birth of their second son, George William Howe, was announced in the *Bury and Norwich Post*, he was born in December 1803 and the birth place is given: Great Witchingham Parsonage. The house was rented.

Dr Bathurst of Christ Church College, Oxford, who became Bishop of Norwich in 1805, had been the non-resident Rector of that Parish. His friend Parson Woodforde of Weston Longville collected the

Witchingham Tithes on his behalf from 1777 to 1786, as "Mr Francis charges him 6d in the Pound for his troubles" [*Diary of a Country Parson* Vol.1. Edited by John Beresford, OUP 1968] "...went to Witchingham and saw Dr Bathurst's Parsonage House the Roof of which is very bad towards the North and some of it down and more falling -- I found Harrison the Tenant very luckily there, as he does not now live in the House, as it is so bad, but he lives at a Brother in Laws at Attlebridge" [Ibid. Vol.II] The tithes were on average £150 p.a. In 1786 Bathurst gave up Witchingham and the new Rector, Mr Jeans (of New College, Oxford), who was also Vicar of St John's Maddermarket, Norwich, moved in with his young wife and lived there for ten years. The house was repaired. Mr and Mrs Jeans were somewhat of a wordly couple, but on good terms with Woodforde, at first. Once, while they were away, on 3rd October 1791 Woodforde went to Witchingham to bury a child "Church not anything like finished repairing yet. We talked a good deal to Mr Jeans' Man William and an Old Woman who takes care of the House during their absence....the House is kept neat and clean." But later Jeans fell out with Woodforde and they parted on bad terms "We have not seen Mr or Mrs Jeans for twelve months past" Woodforde wrote in June 1796 and in October "Mr and Mrs Jeans have left their house and gone to reside in London......They have let their House ready furnished to a Rev'd. Mr Beevor son of Mr James Beevor of Norwich." [Ibid. Vol.IV].

The Rev. Augustus Beevor, who took on some of Jeans's duties, and once conducted a service at Weston Longville where he "was liked very much" [Ibid. Vol.V], was a fiery fellow. Woodforde's Diary for 9th May 1801: "Mr Jeans...is reported to have been at Witchingham for many days and is still there -- Mr Beevor being in the King's Bench Prison and is to continue there for some little time yet for challenging Capt. Pain [to a duel]." Though Beevor returned to Witchingham in July, it can only have been for a few days.
[*NOTE*: Some years later he was in trouble again, in Oct. 1812, when he is described as late of Bergh Apton; he was summoned before the Quarter Sessions in Norwich and charged with assault. The case was not tried until July 1813; he was fined 1/- and discharged. [QS reports NRO C/S1/16]].

Nor was Jeans much better, for the following year Parson Woodforde's Diary has an entry for 7th Jan. 1802: "Mr Foster [of Lenwade] told us that Mr Jeans of Witchingham is in the Kings Bench." It would thus seem that both recent inhabitants of the Witchingham Parsonage had seen the inside of a gaol. By now Woodforde was unwell and 1802 is the last year of his diary. He makes no more mention of Mr Jeans or the Rev. Mr Beevor, nor does he record the arrival of the FitzRoys later in the year.

The Game Duty Lists were published in July, and in July 1802 FitzRoy's name appears against Witchingham. Beevor moved out, and FitzRoy, the Colonel in the Coldstream Guards, moved in. (Was the house still furnished with Mr Jeans's furniture?) The young FitzRoys and their infant son began their Norfolk life. Immediately before their arrival, during the previous month of June, the FitzRoys attended a Masquerade given by Mrs Thellusson (whose husband was MP for Castle Rising) at Foley House in London. [*NOTE*: Foley House with its grounds occupied the space between Mortimer Street and Duchess Street, now occupied by the Langham Hotel. Henry Wheatley, *London Past and Present*, 1891] The Prince of Wales, in the dress of the early 17th century, was one of the 800 guests, with the Dukes of Cumberland and Clarence and Prince William of Gloucester as Dominoes. Mr Dillon and Mr Erskine came as Fashionable Ladies. The event, held to celebrate the General Thanksgiving for the Peace, "possessed a very rare and original combination of magnificence, taste and whim.....the Great Hall converted in to a Village, and at the centre an Inn, at The Sign of the Feathers, Mrs Thellusson the landlady." Other shops included a Post Office, Tap House (Lord Longford an excellent tapster) Levi's Old Clothes Shop (Lord Cranley), Cobbler's Shop (Mr J. Maddocks) and at Snip, the Taylor's Shop, Colonel FitzRoy. [*Norwich Mercury* 5th June 1802] The Prince of Wales went home at 7 in the morning, while others were still there at 11. Though obviously a rather special party, no doubt it was one of many he attended. (Meanwhile at Kempstone the Peace was also celebrated by a Party, the poor of the Parish amounting to about 90 were treated by Mr Johnson and Mr Chamberlain with plenty of roast beef, plum pudding and strong beer "with which they feasted and regaled till evening; when they separated with order and decorum and hearts full of gratitude. In the morning the fragments were divided amongst the largest families." [*Norwich Mercury* 19 June 1802.]).

***

However, early in the following year, 1803, FitzRoy took, or was forced to take, a decision that changed his life.

He was 30, Napoleon was across the Channel once again planning an invasion and in this year alone the British defence forces, which had been recruiting hard since 1793, doubled in size to 500,000 men, [*Cambridge Modern History* Vol.IX.] In March the newspapers published an urgent notice from the War Office calling for all officers of the Army on half pay to make reports of their residences, in case their Services should be called upon. [*Norfolk Chronicle* 19 March 1803]. Indeed every available soldier was needed, it was no time for an ambitious young man to leave the army. FitzRoy was a Lt.Colonel on full pay in the Coldstream Guards [Army Lists PRO Kew], but on the 9th June 1803 he appears in MacKinnon's records [*Origins and Service of the Coldstream Guards*, at Wellington Barracks, London] on half pay in the 85th Regiment of Foot. And here he remained until 5 June 1813 when he was made a Major General.

The most likely explanation for his resignation is ill health. At the time of his service in the Low Countries it was a notoriously unhealthy place, as his cousin Lord Charles confirmed, where hundreds of soldiers contracted fatal diseases and many never fully recovered from the effects of debilitating illnesses such as malaria. FitzRoy was possibly among this number; by the time he arrived at Kempstone five years later it is known that he was physically incapacitated to the extent that he was obliged, on occasion, to use an invalid carriage and to have a bedroom on the ground floor. [See below, description of Kempstone Lodge]. In his letters he makes references to his "old complaint". Galling as it may have been to leave the army at this moment, it did not curtail him completely, for he was still able to ride.

Later that year, in September 1803, there is a newspaper account of him in Windsor Great Park: "His Majesty and Princess Sophia attended by Lady Pitt and Col. FitzRoy took an airing on horseback

15

in the Great Park." [*Norwich and Bury Post* 7th Sep.1803]. *The Norwich and Bury Post*, which reported this, generally paid special attention to the FitzRoy family as a local one of some importance. While there are numerous stories of people falling off carts or horses, drownings, fires and duels, there is no mention of any accident happening to a FitzRoy. Illness, whether contracted in Egypt, the Netherlands, or even dating back to Newcome's School in Hackney, is the most likely explanation.

Unfit to lead men into battle, and released from active military service, FitzRoy accordingly sought a gentler less strenuous occupation. At first he seems to have combined Norfolk life with the army, for the *Bury and Norwich Post* for 15th February 1804 published the following notice: "The Hon. William FitzRoy of Great Witchingham is appointed Aide de Camp to his brother Major General Lord Southampton. It is uncertain, however, if he fulfilled any of the functions of this office. He was in Norwich for the Norfolk Society Fête held in December 1805 at the Assembly Rooms to honour the memory of Nelson." [*Norfolk Chronicle* 21 December 1805.].

***

While at Witchingham he and his wife had three more sons, Arthur William Bagot, born 1805, Charles William Henry Gage, born 1807, and Frederick Thomas William Coke, born 1808. None of these children, nor indeed any FitzRoy, appears in the Great Witchingham register, which is a little incomplete at this time, but a note in the Kempstone register says that his eldest son, William, was baptized in St George's Parish, London [Hanover Square], and that the youngest son was privately baptized at Witchingham in 1808.

***

By 1807 FitzRoy had been introduced to Holkham; it was not for nothing that he named his last born Frederick Thomas William Coke.

The FitzRoys and Cokes had been friends over several generations. The second Duke of Grafton [1683-1757] and Thomas Coke, Earl of Leicester of the first creation [1697-1759] addressed each other by

Thomas William Coke, 1754 - 1842, artist unknown
(Reproduced by kind permission of the Earl of Leicester)

nicknames - the Duke was "The Gran Corteggiano", the Earl "My Angell Trott". [C.W.James, *Chief Justice Coke and his Descendants*, *Country Life* 1929]. I have not found any evidence that Thomas William Coke [1754-1842] and Augustus 3rd Duke of Grafton [1735-1811] were quite as intime, but they certainly saw a great deal of each other and shared the same interests both agricultural and political, along with another good friend and neighbour of theirs, the Earl of Albemarle.

The sight of Holkham Park for FitzRoy, now in his thirties, crippled, perhaps too infirm to even continue as Aide to his brother, and with a wife and the start of a large family to support, was undoubtedly a significant moment in his life. I do not know the date of his first visit, but he may well have been there before. Holkham in the late eighteenth and early nineteenth century was, along with Woburn, at the centre of the agricultural world - it was a place of innovation, where visitors were welcomed and encouraged to admire, examine and learn Coke's farming methods. When FitzRoy observed the Park, planted with thousands of new trees (close always to a FitzRoy's heart), home farm, the neatness, the showmanship with no expense spared and no visible signs of debts or trouble, but lavishness spread thickly, it must have touched his soul. Here, in a mirror image, was the Highgate ferme ornée of his childhood, but extravagantly magnified, that taste which had been his earliest experience made manifest on a breathtaking scale of confidence and security.

In Holkham he recognized the essence of an ordered life, dedication, productivity with virtue, and that tinged with glamour and excitement, not without a pioneering zeal. The possibility of becoming part of that, exchanging the 'security' of the army for association with the Holkham tenantry, (if not quite a member of it), affiliation with Coke, a special relationship, an opportunity to Make Kempstone Perfect with the guidance of His Dear Landlord, must have appeared irresistible.

If this sounds a little extravagant, a little florid, so be it. FitzRoy was a passionate man of great enthusiasm, emotion and impatience; once decided, he entered into the role wholeheartedly.

An event took place in July 1807 which may also have influenced

18

his decision, the death of his mother, the Dowager Baroness Southampton, a widow for ten years. Of her fifteen children she was survived by two daughters, Lady Dungannon and the Hon. Georgiana FitzRoy, and four sons, George Ferdinand 2nd Baron Southampton, General Charles FitzRoy, the Hon Frederick FitzRoy and the Hon. William, the subject of this study. From her will [PRO Prob.ll 1465 q. 625] it appears she was still living at FitzRoy Farm and at a house in Stanhope Street. The main part of her estate went with the title to her eldest son, and to him she left the contents of the two houses, except for her jewels, as well as all the stock live and dead at the Farm. To her second son Charles she left six houses called Pemberton Row in Highgate, now called The Grove, a property her husband had bought from Jacob Preston of Beeston St Lawrence, Norfolk, together with four fields adjoining, Cockshuffle Field, Pear Tree field, Nursery Field and Brook Field. (FitzRoy's youngest son the Rev. Frederick Thomas William Coke FitzRoy was to inherit this property from his Aunt in 1851) - [*County Council Survey of London 1936.*]

William got a piece of ground called the Halfway houses "on the west side of the Road leading from Tottenham Court to Hampstead." There were several houses built on this site, all leased out on long terms. The income from this property is not known, but in his own will drawn up in 1836 he writes of a mortgage on his Camden Town property for £3,000 at 4 per cent. His mother also left him one thousand pounds in Stock in the 3 per cents, two silver Terrines, two silver ladles, a silver tea-pot, and a glass bottle with silver handles. Besides providing a small income, an increase to the half pay he was receiving from the army, the death of a parent can often be the event which marks the beginning of a more settled existence for the children left behind. With the death of his mother, FitzRoy Farm became the property of his elder brother, already altered from the rustic abode of his youth when, in the 1790s, the house had been remodelled by Henry Holland: it was the end of childhood.

In 1811 his brother died, intestate. The heir Charles, 3rd Baron Southampton, lived elsewhere, most probably in Northamptonshire at Whittlebury, for he was certainly there from 1831 onwards. The Dukes of Grafton had lands in Northamptonshire from the 17th century. [Warwick County R.O./ NRA 22981 Bosley and Harper and

NRA 100029 Hastings]. (This Charles, FitzRoy's nephew, married in 1826, his wife died in 1860. There were no children of the marriage. He married again in 1862 and had two sons. In 1865 at the age of 61 he built a huge new house, Whittlebury Lodge. The architect was William Burn. [Mark Girouard, *The Victorian Country House* 1979 Yale, who mistakenly put Whittlebury in Hampshire.]

FitzRoy farm was rented out, and in about 1820, with the metropolis of London creeping ever closer, the house was demolished. The Farmhouse was rebuilt in the twentieth century by Sir Alexander Korda for Vivien Leigh in the mock Tudor style with seven bedrooms. In the park, the farmland, various houses were built. Octavia Hill, social worker and reformer, lived in one of them. Ronald Shiner, the actor, lived in Elm Cottage. The Cottage, another house, is owned by the Emir of Qater [1986] who uses it for members of his staff to live in.

Was FitzRoy not motivated by his mother's memory to make Kempstone perfect? The £6,000 that he spent was almost certainly the bulk of his capital, for, though his account books have not survived, he was not, despite his rather grand life style, a wealthy man. "I have kept too large an establishment to go on without borrowing," he wrote in his will; "I have always kept telling my wife we were living beyond our income, but she turned a deaf ear to it and I am sure she thought me stingy." [see Appendix 3]

And what did Coke think of FitzRoy? In 1807 Coke was 54 and had been widowed for seven years with no sons, though with a beloved youngest daughter. He was compassionate. FitzRoy's family were Whigs, as he was and emotionally too, he may have been moved by the younger man's plight, for he promised FitzRoy a year's lease for every year as long as he, Coke, lived. An agreement was reached: FitzRoy bought the last two years of John Johnson's Kempstone lease and engaged Mr Pond of Dereham to begin the improvements.

A further attraction may have been the proximity of Kempstone to Swaffham, at this period an important centre of social activity. The July races were attended by "a brilliant assembly of company" [*Norwich Mercury* July 1810] and racing was a sport much enjoyed by all FitzRoys. Kempstone to the race course is a distance of no more than six miles, and FitzRoy was several years Steward at the Races.

20

The Races were held over three days and each evening there was dinner with a Ball after. In the winter there was coursing on Swaffham Heath, again attended by "all the world", and cock fighting.

***

But before the FitzRoys moved to their new home, while still at Great Witchingham, four months after the birth of Frederick Thomas William Coke, FitzRoy's wife died. A plaque on the wall of Great Witchingham Church reads "To the Memory of Catherine Haughton wife of Col. the Hon. William FitzRoy youngest brother of George Ferdinand Lord Southampton and only sister to Sir Simon Haughton Clarke Bt. She died on the 16th April 1808 in the thirtieth year of her age and was buried in the family vault at Euston in Suffolk." There follows a poem. From this is can be deduced that the FitzRoys had spent a not inconsiderable amount of their time in Norfolk.

His distress at losing his young wife, mother of their five sons, is recorded again in the church at Euston. This small seventeenth century church has a number of FitzRoy memorials, but not a great many. The plaque to Catherine, on the north wall, is followed by the belief that the anguish of her surviving husband upon this irreparable loss can be softened only by his hope in Christ our Lord.

FitzRoy came then to Kempstone, not only broken in body, but a widower, like his landlord.

***

The land of Kempstone Lodge Farm lay in four different parishes, Kempstone, Beeston, East Lexham and Litcham, which made it complicated in ownership and boundary. The Kempstone parish boundary caused a good deal of trouble when in 1812 the Enclosure took place. The Holkham Audit books record this event with two entries worth quoting: "11th December, paid by cash the Kempstone People, Loss of Time and Expences on going the Bounds in August last £2.13.6."; and of more significance: "Paid by cash their Journeys, Loss of Time and Expences attending the Commissioners at Dereham to give evidence as to the Kempstone Boundary £8.17.8." As the

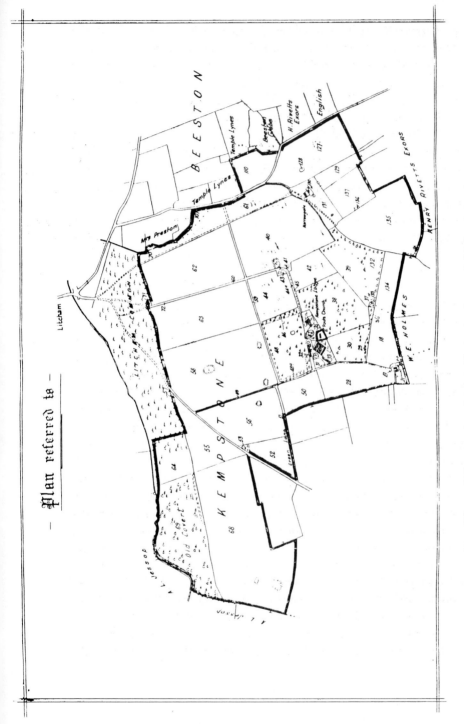

- Plan referred to -

Plan of Kempstone Lodge Farm in the mid 19th century
(In the possession of Mr Rawkins of Kempstone Lodge)

population of Kempstone in 1812 was extremely small and the distance to Dereham little more than seven miles, several journeys must have been needed to get it right. At the same time Kempstone was enclosed, so were seven other parishes on the Holkham Estate, but none of the them excited any entry in the Audit Books. Further complications consisted of various different people owning various different bits of the land that went to make up FitzRoy's farm. Coke kept part of the farm for his own use, while Mr Raven of Litcham owned 4 acres and the Rector of Beeston had two pieces of Glebe land in the Kempstone Field etc. Though gradually Holkham acquired these several small bundles of land, the size and shape of the farm altered somewhat, as pieces were exchanged, taken from or added to the farm next door, which was also on the Holkham estate.

***

The farmhouse at Kempstone had been newly built for John Johnson in 1789 on the site of the Manor Homestall. Before this date William Heard was the capital tenant. He had farmed 430 acres of Kempstone, mostly in field strips, with a further 250 acres which he *owned* intermingled with those he held as a tenant. In 1779 the total acreage of the parish was 836 acres, of which Holkham owned 429, Heard 250, other freeholders 52 and 104 acres of common land. A note on the 1779 Dugmore plan at Holkham says: "A considerable part of Kempstone was open fields but Mr Heard, with the concurrence of Ralph Cauldwell Esq, [the Holkham agent during Lady Leicester's widowhood and executor of Lord Leicester's will], Inclosed the same; but he had not any regard to the division of the Properties, by which means the Baulks are destroy'd, without any Marks being left to the major part of them....the divisions are therefore marked upon the New plan from the Old one which appears (from what remains in the state it was in when it was made) to be very correct...." [Holkham Archives, red plans]. When Heard died in 1788 his land was sold to Holkham and after some further purchases and re-arranegments, two farms were created. Manor Farm, where Heard had lived, was occupied by the Chamberlain family throughout FitzRoy's tenancy and the new house, Kempstone Lodge, appears in the Holkham Audit

Books as "an entire new Farm House, Stables, an addition to the Barn and new Granary and Dovecote over" at a cost of £1,617. In these circumstances, the new building of a farm house, rather than improvements to an existing one, it is slightly unclear how the house and premises were financed. No rent from the tenant is recorded over a number of years, so presumably the rent he would have paid went direct to the builders paying half the costs with Holkham paying the other half. The entry for 1793 reads: "John Johnson his Disbursements for five years building an entire new Farm House £1,617." So it would seem the house and premises actually cost £3,234.

There are further costs over the following years, building a circular wood fence round the House, Fruit Trees, paving a Brewhouse, hanging Paper in 1794 and 1799 etc., though it is never clear exactly what Holkham paid for as an essential and what they considered the tenant should contribute towards. But from an analysis of the Inventory that Blaikie made in 1816 we are able to see what alterations FitzRoy made to the house.

The house built for Johnson was a square double-fronted house with a kitchen etc. at the back; in 1808 it was less than twenty years old.

The move to Kempstone would have been discussed and planned by both FitzRoy and his wife Catherine, and it would seem likely that the alterations started before her death. Though he did improve the farm premises, the bulk of the £6,000 was spent on the house. He changed it from two parlours and four chambers (bedrooms), perfectly adequate for a yeoman farmer, into a mansion suitable for a life lived in the grand manner. Kempstone Lodge was never large, nevertheless by early 19th century standards, before the age of lavish Victorian rebuilding, it probably compared well with the neighbouring houses Lexham Hall (Keppel) or Necton Hall (Mason) and it was made important by FitzRoy. While FitzRoy lived there it was always described by Holkham as a mansion. An indication of his lifestyle can be seen from the description of the house, not so much from the public rooms, but from a room listed in the domestic quarters, the paste room. A paste room was generally found in only very large establishments, (such as Holkham or Euston): it is a kitchen for a specialized pastry cook, though it may also have be the housekeeper's own kitchen where she prepared preserves and medicines. [Rachel Young]. Since FitzRoy entertained a great deal, and more often than not the very grandest people in the country, it was almost certainly used for the former.

Suitable reception rooms were needed for his guests and he had a particular personal need - to have his bedroom on the ground floor. There were also the five little boys to accommodate and several servants.

FitzRoy built new Kitchin [sic] and Offices on to the left of the house, with Nursery and servants' bedrooms above. The old Kitchin he converted into a Dining Room and Library. At the front of the house he built a Porch and a veranda along the length of the house. (Most of this has since been changed.) Inside there were numerous alterations made to accommodate a gentleman and his family, (some of which may have been added to please his second wife a few years later after 1811). By 1816 the rooms on the ground floor in the old house were: the Entrance hall, Dining Room, Drawing Room, Library, Study, Butler's Pantry, China Closet and W.C. To the right of the front door was a Bedchamber, Dressing Room with cloathes Press, Washing Table [fitted dressing table with wash stand], Medicine Closet, Glass Case for guns and window seat. This was Fitz Roy's own room; sleeping on the ground floor and not attempting the struggle of going upstairs, together with the new Invalid Stable described in the Audit Books [1808] on the south side of the Barn, the cost of which Holkham contributed to, plus references [see below] in his letters to late rising (a sure sign of someone who is in pain and sleeps badly) confirm his crippled state.

The new part "built from the ground" consisted of a Kitchin, Scullery, Larder, Paste Room, Housekeeper's room, Servants Hall [dining room], Servants Dressing room, Trunk room, Game Larder and Servants Keeping Room [sitting room]. Again not all of this addition has survived for commodious new "Offices" became increasingly common later in the century, when they sometimes grew to be as extensive as the house they served. The Servants' Dressing Room was for the menservants' livery. FitzRoy had a Butler, Thomas Buckley, from 1814, or before, to 1836 when Buckley died, [Kempstone Registers NRO.] and footmen. His wife had a Lady's

Maid, whose room is listed upstairs. Also upstairs were five bedrooms and a bathroom, made from a loft, with a shower bath and warm booth.

There is no list of how many bedrooms there were in the new part of the house. FitzRoy was very up to date with the Mod. Cons. The first *efficient* W.C. was patented in 1778, the water for it, and for the bathroom, very probably came from a tank in the roof. [Rachel Young] Between the servants' quarters and the "Best part of the house" were green baize doors and along the passage, by the Candlestick Closet near the Butler's Pantry, a row of bells to summon footmen or parlourmaids to a particular room.

FitzRoy put in a good many new fireplaces, marble ones in the main reception rooms and in his bedroom; in any other room that needed better heating, a Register Stove. He renewed many of the windows, fixing new locks and shutters, shelves in the Library and numerous cupboards. These permanent fixtures he left as "Heirlooms to the Estate". The house also had a wine cellar.

***

"I have no wish to hide anything from my Landlord, I have kept most accurate Acc[ounts] of all I have Expended and Received since I have been at Kempstone" FitzRoy wrote in one of his marathon letters to Blaikie on 4th December 1816, "which is open to Your Inspection at all times........I paid Mr Pond and his Executors 6,000£ for the Improvements to the House, Stables and Church, including Dog Kennel and two Gates. Estimate was 3,000£."

The Dog Kennel, with dogs' troughs and beds, a copper and furnace, would have been suitable for a pack of hounds. At that time there were several private packs in Norfolk, not just Fox hounds, but Stag hounds, Harriers, Beagles and Otter Hounds, sometimes owned by people living in other counties. Later, in the 1830s, FitzRoy was a Joint Master of the West Norfolk Fox Hounds. [*Norfolk Chronicle* and *Bailey's Hunting Directory*].

***

Kempstone Lodge, front view (Photo Alan Sanders)

Kempstone Lodge, rear view (Photo Alan Sanders)

Of the farm buildings Blaikie's survey records that FitzRoy had built: a poultry building, piggery, slaughter house, cow house, bulls house, calf pen, horse shed, Bailiff's stable, cart shed, waggon lodge and carpenter's shop. The cost of these did not come into the £6,000; they were put up by FitzRoy after 1808 before 1816, some newly built, others repaired, and at his own expense, "...had they originally been properly done [they] would not have required repairs....The new Piggery and other alterations made this year *entirely* at my *own Expense.*" [Letter 2]. Blaikie must have been of the opinion that they were virtually rebuilt as he describes them as "new" in his report. There is a partial account of them in the Audit Books for 1808 and 1809, for this is the £687 mentioned in the opening paragraph e.g. William Nichols bricklayer building a new "Hoggery", Invalid Stable on the South side of Barn and fence Walls on the North side of Barn £47. 18. 8. etc. It is therefore possible to add a considerable amount to the £6,000.

At this period of his life, FitzRoy appears to have had a rather cavalier attitude to money, evidenced by the hundred per cent difference between Mr Pond's estimate and his bill. It is comforting to note that nineteenth century builders overstepped estimates, as can happen today, but to double it seems a little careless and the unfortunate experience with his first bailiff (see below) shows that FitzRoy was not attending to his financial affairs as closely as he could have done. Certainly by 1816 his approach had undergone a change, he was keeping the accounts mentioned in the above letter and when he wished to build a Garden Wall, at a cost of £200, he applied to Holkham to pay for it.

***

In 1808 Coke had 55 Norfolk tenants who paid over £100 a year in rent, John Barker at Dunton paying the highest at £1,010, Thomas Dewing at Castle Acre next with £668; and there were several who paid less than £100. 15 out of the 17 Buckinghamshire tenants paid rents between £175 and £582. The latter all had leases of one year, while the Norfolk tenants had, in the main, leases of 21 years. FitzRoy's rent was £351, and his lease, or lack of it, (the agreement that it was to go from year to year as long as Coke lived) was to cause him some anxiety. This was partly his own fault, and partly his unique position on the Estate. In order for FitzRoy to be An Uncommon Tenant, he did not, could not, have a lease, for no lease meant, in effect, freedom and independence for him to farm as he chose, unrestricted and uninterfered with, a suitable arrangement for a gentleman. He was given the shooting rights over the farm, as has been noted, and further, he was exempt from the carting work required from other tenants and the need to keep dogs. "I have never had any lease made out, but so firm a Reliance have I of Mr Coke's Integrity, that I felt as comfortable and secure as if I had it in my possession signed and sealed........and it was that which Induced me to lay out so much money on the House etc." [Letter 12]. This unofficial arrangement lasted for nearly twenty years, but by 1826 when Blaikie, Coke's agent, explained to him that such a running lease on an entailed Estate could not possibly be legal, if only because of the risks to both parties, FitzRoy had long since decided that he would anyway prefer to have a lease such as the other Holkham tenants had, despite the cost and the conditions. [Letter 83]. The standard Holkham lease of this period, a draft of which had been drawn up by Blaikie in 1817 and was subsequently used with very little variation for each tenant, demanded a lengthy number of conditions in order to enforce a high standard of cultivation, proper maintenance of the buildings and detailed attention to care of the trees and hedges etc. as well as full protection for the Landlord including penalties against non compliance.

**

From the begining FitzRoy employed a bailiff to run the farm, which was to be done on Holkham lines, but with a greater licence, so that he would be able to spend large parts of the year away on visits.

The cost of building a brand new cottage for the bailiff has already been recorded, though FitzRoy was re-paying Holkham for it at a rate of 10% p.a. Again, the employment of a bailiff denoted FitzRoy's special status, other tenants being committed to their farms twelve months a year, though by the middle of the century some had

The bailiff's cottage at Kempstone today (Photo Alan Sanders)

stewards. [Holkham Audit Books] In July 1808, highly recommended by various neighbours, John Prentice entered FitzRoy's service, as bailiff, at a salary of £100 a year, plus perquisites. He was in a position of considerable responsibility for he received and paid all the monies needed for the farm and when he asked FitzRoy for extra money, the better to improve the concern, he was given it. However, despite his reputation as "a person of the strictest honesty" he was far from it, and almost from his first day at Kempstone, began a systematic plan to defraud and deceive. His method was very simple, entering large sums of money in his account book as Paid, when they were not, he pocketed the cash. By the time he was found out, in November 1809, he had managed to steal over £700. Prentice's defence was that he arrived at Kempstone deeply in debt and had used the money to these ends; but he was also found guilty of slandering FitzRoy, asserting that his master was a "damnable gambler" who never gave him sufficient cash to run the farm, among other un-recorded insults. Prentice was taken before a magistrate on 27th November 1809 and tried at the Quarter Sessions at Holt on 19th January 1810. At the start he pleaded guilty, but then changed his mind and petitioned the Court to assign him a Counsel; the Court directed Mr Alderson, a relative of Mrs Opie, to defend him. A number of local merchants gave evidence against Prentice; he owed money to all of them. Despite Alderson's attempts to claim that the Quarter Sessions had no power to try such an offence, and that FitzRoy had been inaccurately described as "the Hon Wm. FitzRoy, whereas he should have been called William FitzRoy Esq., commonly called the Honourable William FitzRoy" and other legal quibbles, Prentice was found guilty and sentenced to be transported for 7 years "and for that purpose to be conveyed to the Castle at Norwich." Among the Magistrates at Holt was Frederick Keppel Esq., FitzRoy's neighbour at Lexham, and the Rev. Dixon Hoste of Tittleshall. The newspaper account ends with a note that the prisoner "had every possible mercy extended towards him by the prosecutor [FitzRoy] ......who had destroyed two forged receipts to save the prisoner's life." [Quarter Sessions notebooks NRO C/S1/16 and the *Norfolk Chronicle* 29th Jan.1810]

The last sentence of this report is the most significant, and not an exaggeration. At this date and until 1832, forgery carried the death penalty; and though if convicted Prentice might have had his sentence commuted on appeal to transportation, (probably for life, or at least fourteen years instead of seven) equally he may have been less fortunate and met his end, hung ("executed") on the Castle hill in Norwich.

Why FitzRoy chose to save him from this fate can only be a matter for conjecture. Possibly on the battlefield he had seen enough of violent and unnatural death. Possibly he considered transportation a sufficient punishment; for a man of Prentice's standing and education, the ordeal of hard labour in a prison hulk while waiting for the long journey to Australia or Van Dieman's Land would have been extremely hard, and the likelihood of his ever returning was remote. Whether Prentice had a wife and family to plead for him is also unknown. The most likely truth is a combination of all three.

***

FitzRoy took part in Norfolk life, at least from the time he took up residence at Kempstone. He sat on the Jury of the Assizes at Thetford, was a Trustee of the short-lived Anchor Fire Office (at the Back of the Inns in Norwich, fellow Trustees included Lord Albemarle and Lord Townshend), was a steward at the Swaffham Races and, with two exceptions, attended the Sheep Shearings at Holkham each year from 1807 to 1821. The Sheep Shearing meetings were held over three or four days in late June, and were used by Coke as a means of making known his farming methods. By the early 1800s they were major agricultural events, rivalling the Duke of Bedford's at Woburn, and were often attended by the same interested and important people. [R.A.C. Parker, *Coke of Norfolk*, OUP 1976.] Visitors came from every part of England and many from abroad. HRH The Duke of Sussex, the Dukes of Grafton and Bedford, the Earl of Albemarle, the American Ambassador, and several Russian Princes were among those invited to stay in the house for the event, as was FitzRoy. Each morning parties of the distinguished guests were shown over the Holkham farms and those of the neighbouring tenants; once, in 1806, they went as far as Lexham to see the water meadows there.

32

[*Norwich Mercury*, 28 June 1806]. Various animals were on display, competing for prizes, and to complete the emphasis on the superior quality of the wool, the Herrings exhibited their Norwich shawls.

[*NOTE*: The fashion for wearing shawls began in the late eighteenth century; made of the finest local wool and laboriously hand decorated, Norwich shawls used patterns based on Indian designs and were not only colourful but above all warm, important at a time when women's dresses were made of the lightest fabrics, muslin and lawn.]

In 1801 a model of a threshing machine was shown. Entries for the competitions were not restricted to the tenantry: Col. Keppel of East Lexham won the prize for water meadows in 1813, Mr Powell of Snettisham's Boar Pig won first prize in 1817 and in the same year the prize for the greatest number of lambs alive on the 1st June went to Mr Wright of Stanhoe. In 1808, his first year as a tenant, FitzRoy won a silver cup valued at 10gns for the best 2 year old New Leicester wether.

Every afternoon 350 or more sat down to dinner in the house, which was followed by speeches, numerous toasts (the most frequent being Coke's own "Live and let Live") and sometimes a song or two. These huge dinners were cheerful occasions when not only new implements or the results of experimental farming methods were discussed, such as Coke reporting in 1809 that working oxen "did not answer", but were also opportunities for a certain amount of jovial letting down of hair. In July 1815, after dinner on the second day, FitzRoy rose and was reported as saying: "As one of Mr Coke's worst tenants, it might be presumptuous in him to put himself forward on this occasion; however he trusted, with such good example before his eyes, he would improve and took occasion to thank Mr Coke in handsome terms for the advantages he had received from his advice and instruction." [*Norfolk Chronicle* 8th July 1815]. This was not false modesty. [For a list of his Holkham prizes see Appendix 2].

FitzRoy was also a member of the Norfolk Agricultural Society (president T.W.Coke) and on the committee: in 1810 he visited the Agricultural Fête at Woburn. He was a guest of honour at the celebration dinner for Charles James Fox's birthday held in February 1819 at the Norwich Assembly Rooms, where one of the toasts drunk was to "Admiral Ludkin and the Wooden Walls of old England".

[*Norwich Courier*, 7th February 1819] In short he lived the life of the Norfolk gentry and ran with the landed classes, differing only from them by not being the owner of his farm.

***

In July 1811 he married for a second time. Three weeks before the marriage he attended a Fête given by the Prince Regent at Carleton House on 17th June, with the Townshends, Walpoles, Jerninghams etc. On 4th July he was married by special licence at St.George's, Hanover Square, to his first cousin, Lady Elizabeth FitzRoy, the 3rd daughter of his uncle, the Duke of Grafton. Her father had died four months before the marriage, in March 1811, leaving her, as an unmarried daughter, a considerable "dot" of £17,000. The honeymoon, if there was one, was short, for at the end of July FitzRoy was back in Norfolk, at Dereham, for the Anniversary meeting of the Norfolk Agricultural Society at which he shared a prize for his water meadows with Mr Thomas Purdy of Castle Acre.

***

Lady Elizabeth FitzRoy was 35 years old at the time of her marriage, two years younger than her cousinly husband. There were to be no children of this union, but on marriage she became step-mother to the five little boys, the eldest of whom was 9 and the youngest 3. There is no evidence of how she settled into this new and difficult, though not unusual, role; but from her will and that of FitzRoy's the boys certainly grew to call her Mother, for when Fitz Roy leaves his eldest son, William, "his mother's portrait" he is referring to a picture by Hoppner of Lady Elizabeth FitzRoy, not of Catherine Haughton Clarke. Lady Elizabeth also shows concern in her will to leave the children well provided for - they were all FitzRoys.

***

In March 1816 Thomas William Coke engaged a new agent to deal with the day to day running of the Holkham Estate. He was Francis

Lady Elizabeth FitzRoy, painting by Hoppner, 1810
(By kind permission of the Duke of Grafton)

Blaikie, the much-famed steward of Lord Chesterfield who had recently died. The previous agent, Crick, had been paid £300 a year, but for Blaikie, a man of great ability, experience and dedication, his salary began at £550. One of his first innovations was to begin the Letter Books, a custom which lasted until the advent of the typewriter, though after 1832, the year Blaikie retired, they are never quite as interesting again. The idea was to record all letters received at the Holkham estate office and all those written from it. The books contain a good proportion of the letters, but by no means all, and in the case of FitzRoy very often extracts only. FitzRoy's undoubted invalidity gave him an added opportunity to write at length and this he did.

Blaikie arrived at Holkham in March and began recording letters straight away, but the first five from FitzRoy, written between March and October, are addressed not to Blaikie, but to his "Dear Landlord" Thomas William Coke. As four of them are marked "Extract only", they must have contained news of a more personal kind as well as matters concerning the Estate. A note from Coke written from London and dated May 1816, thanks FitzRoy for "all your Kind letters". FitzRoy discussed all aspects of his farming with Coke. His letter dated 30th March 1816 plunged straight into a concern which was to take up a good deal of time and patience, the fate of two tumble down cottages which had belonged to his predecessor, Johnson, now dead, and FitzRoy's attempt to buy them for £80 from Johnson's executors. He was obliged to negotiate through Mr Yarrington, a Swaffham solicitor of immense slowness. FitzRoy told Coke: "I have particularly kept your name out of the enquiry knowing that they w'd put on more if they thought you wanted it, they [the cottages] certainly ought to belong to you as you have land on three sides of them..... The cottages are not worth repairing" and added both he and his neighbour Mr Chamberlain, of the Manor Farm, Kempston, were sadly off for cottages for their labourers, and he records how Chamberlain has often asked FitzRoy to petition Coke to build some. He mentioned that Lady Elizabeth FitzRoy had written to Coke on this matter in 1814 and Crick, the previous agent, had promised some improvement. So far nothing had happened. Crick is often quoted in FitzRoy's letters, usually referring to something he had promised, such as a Black-smith's shop. [Letter 67]. On that occasion Crick had got as far as measuring out the ground for the shop and even procured the materials to build it with, until they were diverted into some other project.

***

In common with most, FitzRoy liked to claim that the farm had been in a very poor state at the beginning of his tenancy, but as Johnson had won several prizes at the Sheep Shearings for his animals this cannot have been altogether true. Certainly the creation of water meadows was much encouraged on the whole Estate and FitzRoy wished to pull down those two cottages in order to do just that. Where previously land had been foul and useless, or in this case inhabited by cottages "tumbling down, roof fallen in", water meadows were a great im-provement. Between 1808 and 1816 FitzRoy clayed 200 acres of land, out of his total farm of 400 acres. [Letter 4].

In 1816 he had 15 acres of Yellow Scotch Turnips, all doing well, but his swedes on heavy land were not so good and he is convinced they prefer light soil. He has also experimented with drilling seed against the more old fashioned way of broadcasting, trying out both methods in the same field and invites Coke to judge: "when you come here you will be the umpire." "Jay versus Fitz Roy" he quotes. (Jay his Bailiff).

At a Holkham Sheep Shearing dinner in 1819 he recounted the result of this story by way of amusing the guests. "The General returned his thanks [his health had been drunk], and bore with ample testimony of his experience to the superiority of the drill husbandry. He recited a case similar to the one often told by his Hon. Friend (Mr Coke) that when he found himself at leisure to beat his sword into a ploughshare (applause) he had a worthy, but very obstinate man for a bailiff - an industrious steady, hard working, prejudiced broad-cast-man (laughter) He had with this man repeated disputes, and many bloodless battles; but he felt great respect for his integrity, he (the gallant General) almost every day submitted to the lie direct. At Length he hit upon a scheme that was likely to bring the matter to an issue; he appointed a field to decide the quarrel, and gave the sturdy champion of old-fashioned prejudices a formal challenge, that he should take one half and himself the other, and cultivate, cleanse, manure, sow and reap it, and measure and market the produce separately. Not to tire the company, the result was so completely in favour of the drill, that the bailiff yielded the victory, and not only so, but became a partizan on the opposite side." [*Norwich Mercury* June 1819].

This experiment was significant enough to find its way into the Holkham Book of Observations 1801-1858. This collection is in a small scrap book, far more humble and irregular than the title suggests. However, it must have been of some moment since FitzRoy recounted the story in 1819 while the event took place in 1815. The point is that Jay, described as "the *most prejudiced* man *possible*", is forced to concede that the sample from the drilled or mown wheat [sic] is worth 1/- more per coomb than the other. An irrefutable proof. Undoubtedly stung by his unfortunate experience with Prentice, FitzRoy had chosen the elderly Jay as bailiff precisely for his very conservative and reliable ways.

By the end of August 1816 FitzRoy was ready to harvest the corn, but Jay "wouldn't let me begin Harvest these 10 days, he says the corn is *too green*, and he is sure you and those who cut so green *spoil* your sample. In answer I say, Then why do they continue such a practice?" Jay had presumably replaced Prentice as FitzRoy's Bailiff. In this letter, written to Coke his landlord and mentor, FitzRoy's enthusiasm continues with an account of a private venture into agricultural experimentation of a more radical kind.

Using what he describes as an old piece of Pasture, he divided it up into four half-acre plots and fertilized it in four different ways, noting the cost of each. The most expensive method, using pulverised oil cake, cost £3, including the carriage of the said cake, while the method used for the fourth piece cost nothing it was, as he writes: "dare I name it ? folded with Sheep." The date is noted 25th August 1816 and which piece, he asks, will be best on 25th August 1817 ?

It is unlikely that Blaikie, a methodical Scot of exemplary behaviour, perfect manners and an overwhelming devotion to his duty, found FitzRoy easy to deal with. FitzRoy was not an ordinary tenant, he had no lease, and he loved writing letters; not only did he write at length, but frequently. Only once in the course of their 16 year relationship did Blaikie permit himself a written criticism of FitzRoy·

in 1828 in a letter to Stokes, the Fakenham solicitor, he wrote of theGeneral's "whims and fancies" and told Stokes that FitzRoy was not very punctual in his payments. [Letter 102].

It is very hard to know if the penalties listed in the Holkham leases were ever enforced. Failure to look after hedges could result in a fine of forty shillings per rod, for cutting down trees without written permission a fine of £20, and for mowing meadow lands two years in succession without improving them tenants could be fined £50 an acre. R.A.C.Parker in his book *Coke of Norfolk, A Financial and Agricultural Study* agrees that they were probably not insisted upon and gives an example of a tenant, Gibbs, who could have been fined £1,500, but he says there are no signs that either Gibbs or any other tenant was ever fined, at least not in the courts. Tenants were bound to the four-course system, (though some had five or six courses) and by 1816 FitzRoy had adopted his own slightly more complicated variation. The Norfolk four-course system was one fourth part sown with Turnip Seeds, to be twice hoed, and then fed off and consumed as far as possible by sheep, one fourth part sown with Barley, one fourth part grass mown only once in the same year and pastured by cattle and sheep and the last fourth part to be corn or grain. [Holkham lease]. Both Blaikie and Coke were in the habit of riding over the farms from time to time, inspecting them, so that even if fines were never enforced, they remained a possibility and it would be a foolish tenant who did not observe the basic provisions of his lease. The farms bordering what is now the A1065 in Castle Acre and Lexham were seen perhaps more than most, as they lay on the route to London: not unnaturally Coke observed the state of their hedges as he passed and reported on them to Blaikie.

Blaikie needed to employ all the tact and wisdom he could muster when addressing FitzRoy. However, Blaikie loved a challenge, and he was extremely tenacious. It is hard to believe from reading the Holkham Letter Books, on numerous other far more awkward subjects, that Blaikie shied from difficult situations; indeed he appears to have relished them.

FitzRoy's first recorded letter to Blaikie [Letter 6] was written on 3rd October 1816, in the third person. It is a request for some draining tiles, "or what they call in this county gutterbricks, to make an underdrain from the yards to prevent water injuring the foundations of walls etc........An answer under cover to Lord Charles FitzRoy MD Kempstone Lodge, Rougham, will sure to be safely delivered to General FitzRoy." FitzRoy had been at Holkham in July of that year for the Sheep Shearing, when Blaikie was presented with a premium (which he declined with great modesty) for his invention of a horse-hoe. [*Norfolk Chronicle*, 13 July 1816]. They must have met on this occasion, if not before. Nevertheless he addresses Blaikie as though he were a tradesman. Presumably he asked Blaikie to reply to Lord Charles FitzRoy because he himself was away. The inclusion of Rougham in the address is because Rougham was the nearest post office, and there was also a Money Order Office there. Letters were also frequently sent by messenger.

Blaikie, in his characteristic way replied by return, addressing Fitz-Roy as "Honourable Sir", a mode he was never to vary: "In answer to your application for Building materials of yesterday's date, I will (as is my Duty) lay your request before Mr Coke, and I purpose waiting upon you with this answer - on Tuesday morning next - about nine o'clock."

In 1816, his first year at Holkham, Blaikie was much engaged with his Report on the Estate, inspecting each farm and drawing up the inventories of fixtures and fittings in every building owned by the Estate. To reach Kempstone by nine in the morning he would have to leave Holkham before seven, or else be staying in the neighbourhood.

FitzRoy's second letter to Blaikie [Letter 8] on 9th Nov. 1816, again written in the third person, "General FitzRoy presents his compliments to Mr Blaikie", records that he has sent the cuttings of the Irish Ivy, with which part of Kempstone Church was covered, and "is happy he [FitzRoy] has it in his power to send any thing from Kempstone to Holkham." In FitzRoy's next letter, dated six days later, he addresses Blaikie as "Sir" by January 1818 has moved on to "Dear Sir," and by July 1822 such progress has been made that he now greets him as "My Dear Blaikie". This is not surprising in the light of Coke's regard for Blaikie, who by 1819 thought of him more as a friend than an employee.

By December 1816 FitzRoy had heard of Blaikie's report on his farm, even if he hadn't yet read it. "I have every reason to be pleased and gratified. The more so as I am well aware you speak your opinion manfully - without prejudice, or partially, [sic] and also I know you are a competent judge." This letter [Letter 12] which FitzRoy himself describes as "Voluminous", is worth quoting in part, for it would seem once FitzRoy had an inkling that Blaikie approved of his farm he needed to pour out his ideas and explanations:

".....I purchased the two unexpired years of the late Johnson's lease of his Executors - after the Expiration of that Period my Rent was Raised, and it was agreed that I was to have 21 Years *Renewable* every year as long as Mr Coke lives.......I have to lament much that I did not know of your coming to Inspect my farm as I should have been up and should have had great pleasure in Riding over my farm with you, as you would have pointed out to me what you thought best to be done, I am perfectly without any prejudice, and shall always gladly follow any plans you may suggest, my sole wish is to please Mr Coke and meet his wishes in every thing........Your remark respecting part of my land wanting Claying is very just, I regularly Clay from 20 to 30 Acres annually according to Circumstances. I keep a regular Book Account of the years each field is clayed, and of course as all cannot be done at once, it must take time to go regularly through the business which has been much protracted by the *foul state* I found the farm in when I first took it, and also by my having so much Carting for Buildings and Roads - which will also account for some of the shabby old Cart Horses you must have seen upon my farm, old worn out Hunters and Hacks.

From the quantity of grass land I have in proportion to Arable it was deemed by old Mr Beck of Lexham that the four course cropping was the best adapted to my farm, which Mr Coke also approved of. I enclose You herewith my plan which I keep regularly entered in a book.

I should much like you to see the plan or map of my farm as it *was*, You will see how I have put aside useless and bad Fences, I take great pains with my Fences, and in a few years more I shall have compleated them. I have some plans in my head which I should like to point out to you when you have leisure to give me a day for these matters.......Your Remark respecting the Chancell of the Church is perfectly Correct, it is very dangerous, and if the Lay Rector (Mr

41

Coke) does not *soon* repair it, it will come down and cost him much money to rebuild it - I laid out 200£ on the improvement of the Interior of the Church.

The Ivy is a Great ornament, and the Church standing Higher than the adjoining and surrounding Ground, and having a very deep ditch round it, with the additional care of opening the Doors regularly to admit a Current of air, it is always dry, and not damp from the Ivy - which will not be permitted to grow luxuriantly, as to Endanger the walls from damp, besides the foregoing attention to keep the Church dry there is a fire made in Winter time, which not only makes the Church dry, but warm --

I am perfectly of your opinion respecting the Kitchin and Fruit Garden wanting a wall, and also that is more a convenience to the Occupier than a benefit for the Estate. Except that on some *future* day it may be very acceptable to perhaps some branch of the Holkham Family who may reside at Kempston and will not be sorry to have good fruit on their table.

A Cart Shed is *absolutely necessary*, there never having been one Erected when the farm buildings were done, and Mr Crick promised there should be one, there is no place to put a Cart, Roller, Plough or any other Implement undercover - not so much shed as there is on all smaller farms, one would have been granted when the farm buildings were first built but I had not made up my mind where it was to be placed.

Mr Coke having kindly acceeded to my proposal of building a Garden Wall and Cart Shed at the Back, sets that matter at rest, and the seven and a half per cent I shall think no heavy burden to my Rent and shall as soon as spring arrives begin my operation, and all it costs me above 200£ I shall gladly pay out of my own pocket, and should it cost less (which it will not) of course have less addition to my Rent than 15£ which addition is to commence from Michaelmas 1817 I have bespoke bricks and Lyme etc.

The stock on my Farm has been selected with great care Expense and attention, I changed the Leicester Flocks for South Downs and the Home bred Cows for Devons. In short I have throughout had but one view which was to meet Mr Coke's wishes in Every thing, and continue to do so as long as I possess Kempstone.

42

I must apologize for this long statement and remain Sir yours etc.ect.
P.S. I always insure every year. " [Letter 12].

Before moving on to his account of farming, which he had enclosed with this letter, it is interesting to note FitzRoy's idea that he was setting a precedent at Kempstone and that he believed in the future his successors would be a Coke, or some other relation. By contrast it is a little strange that for eight years, for want of a shed, farm implements had been kept out of doors, open to the elements, though this may have been an exaggeration. As to the stock, the change to different breeds was not recent, FitzRoy had had South Down sheep from the start of his tenancy, if not before. According to the *Norwich Mercury* for June 1807 FitzRoy was at the Holkham Sheep Shearings showing 10 South Down Theaves, which he sold there for £47. At the 1808 Shearings FitzRoy won prizes for Leicester wethers, probably animals he had bought from Johnson who had won prizes in the same category the year before, and in 1809 FitzRoy showed both Leicesters and South Downs. Coke had changed to South Downs in the 1790's. At the 1814 Shearings FitzRoy showed a Devon Bull, which got a special mention, though the prize for this class went to Mr Reeve of Wighton.
But to continue......

"General FitzRoy's mode of Cropping His Farm
Supposing it to be Michaelmas.

No 1 -- One fourth of my arable land is Artificial Grass, half of which red Clover mown once, and folded off by sheep (the lambs) same as Turnips are fed off --
The other half is White Clover and trufoil fed by the Flocks (which are folded there at nights) and not mown --
No 2   One fourth Turnips
No 3   One fourth Wheat Stubble and Pea Stubble and Oat Stubble
No 4   One fourth Barley Stubble half laid down with Red Clover and half with white Clover and Trufoil --
The First, No 1, the Half that is Red Clover is ploughed up and drilled with Wheat.

The other half is reserved till Spring and is Clayed during the Winter time then sub-divided into two parts. The Strong land is sown with Oats the Light with Peas, it all comes in the Year following for Turnips with the Wheat Stubble.

The second, No 2, is Turnips and is fed off with Sheep and in the spring sown with Barley and Artifical Grass Seeds half Red Clover and half White and Trefoil.

The Third, No 3, is Wheat Pease or Oat Stubble.

The Fourth, No 4, is Barley Stubble with new layer half Red Clover, half White Clover and Trefoil, the Red Clover will be mown for Hay, the White Trefoil fed with Sheep so that only once in eight years I grow Red Clover and only once in eight years mow for Hay, Wheat or Red Clover Layer or Stubble.

Turnips
Barley
White Clover or Trefoil
Peas or Oats
Turnips
Barley
Red Clover
Wheat
Turnips
Barley
White Clover etc.etc.etc..

Wheat once in 8 years Peas or Oats once in 8 years Turnips and Barley every 4th Year, Red Clover once in 8 years White Clover and Trefoil once in 8 years."

Blaikie's answer confirmed the arrangement for building the Wall and in an almost confiding vein, he wrote: ".....your recent written detail which you have done me the honour to leave at this place during my absence on Estate business.....I humbly thank you for your flattering approbation, or what you are pleased to call my manly conduct, in boldly giving me an impartial opinion on the general subject of the cultivation and management, and the Individual occupation of the lands - upon Mr Cokes superb, far famed and justly celebrated Estate. From you Sir, I acknowledge I expected no less than I have found, the liberal declaration of a Gentleman -- But from a mere Farmer I expect to be looked upon in a very different light -- Their opinion (although I will not say I set it at naught) yet this I will say, that no publick or private opinion inconsiderately taken up ever bias me to tend to make me swerve from what (after mature consideration) I consider to be my proper line of duty. But I fear this egotism is unbecoming in me, while it is offensive to you -- I will therefore solicit your forgiveness -- and subscribe myself Honoured Sir, yours etc.etc.."

***

Anxious to explain why he had written his "Voluminous Letter" FitzRoy wrote again at once: "....I should not have troubled my self to have written had you been at Holkham, as I would have, in person, in a few minutes, Explained all therein Contained, but you being then in Buckinghamshire.....my endeavour ever since I have occupied Kempstone is to meet Mr Coke's wishes in *every* thing concerning this place, independent of the personal Love and Attachment I feel towards him, my respect and admiration of his publick character would induce me to act in every way most pleasing to him - Every one who knew this place - when I first took it can bear Testimony to the State it was in, and to the improvements I have made in every part... though we are cruelly off for Cottages."

***

And the following day 29th December 1816 FitzRoy wrote yet another letter, this time on the receipt of Blaikie's: "I have only this Eve received your letter.......about the Garden Wall....I am struck by your manly and business like manner of stating the agreement, it, as you justly remark prevents after reckonings and explanations - which are always unpleasant - I wish every one I have business to transact with, had been as open, and as candid and as manly as yourself - it would have been pounds in my pocket, besides the disagreeable altercations that I have been obligded to enter into frequently. [He was probably referring to his property in Camden Town, the Halfway Houses] You

45

certainly never dictate to me the Terms, they come spontaneously from myself, but I would not think it precumption [sic] on your part - if at any time you will point out to me wherein I may be wrong, I shall feel obliged and flattered by your advice, the advice of a competent judge - and an Honest man must be acceptable to every one of common sense - Your not having written to me sooner requires no apology whatever - I am well aware of the multitude of business you must have on your hands - and cannot be so selfish as to expect I am to be the only one who is to engross all your time and thought.

"I am gratified to Mr Coke for his kindness in acceeding [sic] to my wishes indeed I wrote to him last May to thank him - all shall be done in a workmanlike manner and all particulars as stated, or rather recapitulated in your letter, shall be attended to, I fear it [the Wall] will not come to under 200£ I have made up my mind to add 100£ to it but you shall see the whole in black and white when compleated --

"I wish I had your art of writing. I have never rec'd a more satisfactory letter than the one I received from you this day, it gave me real pleasure, it is not one word too little, not one word too much - I speak my mind, and all I can say is, I never more rejoiced at any one circumstance than I did - when I heard Mr Coke had secured your services - I wrote to him to congratulate him on the event, at the time, for tho' I did not know you by sight, I had frequently heard of you from several people, and from Ld. Chesterfield himself, with whom I was very intimate - and since I have known you, I am sure I have had no reason to alter my opinion - Mr Coke wanted an upright man, whose integrity - was not to be intimidated and who would badly correct abuses - which were getting a head too fast by all accounts in every department at Holkham, I cannot this letter conclude without thanking you for your open and manly conduct towards me as a tenant & so just and proper towards Mr Coke as my *Friend* and Landlord."

***

This was the last letter FitzRoy wrote to Blaikie in the year 1816; even allowing for the extravagant way in which people addressed each other in the early nineteenth century, "high Georgian English", FitzRoy had evidently decided that Blaikie was a man to be trusted and one with whom he could conduct his farming business. However no letters of this kind can truly be relied upon to give an accurate portrait of a character, especially considering the times. To the modern reader these letters may seem ponderous and repetitive, more the kind one might receive from a lawyer, but in the early nineteenth century, with infrequent meetings between the people involved, no telephone, faxes or even telegrams it was essential to convey exact meaning in the strictest terms and, as far as possible, eliminate the need for questions. While some seem over effusive, an easy flowing sort of prose that contains no criticism, when there *are* matters to be questioned or points to be emphasised the language has a sternness about it which, out of context, can seem moderately offensive in its reproval. Courtesy, always essential, takes on an almost sarcastic mode when the subject of the letter is being reminded that he has or has not fulfilled a request. Nevertheless despite careful wording and general absence of ambiguity, misunderstandings did sometimes arise.

It was important to acknowledge receipt of a letter and to quote the date of the letter to which a reply was being made, since the possibility of its not reaching its destination was always present. Blaikie encouraged the practise of sending letters by reliable messengers, and this was, despite Rougham, the method most frequently employed, though by 1828 FitzRoy was using some kind of official postal service ".....we seldom send to the post of a Monday as there is no London post on that day" [Letter 106] and in 1833 he writes "...this letter was put in the Kempstone Box on the 23rd July but by some mistake was over looked [until the 1st August]." [Letter 111].

Absolute accuracy, at least to Blaikie, was all important and he generally succeeded in communicating his meaning with great clarity, allowing no possible room for doubt. It was important also, as Blaikie knew, to keep letters in a safe place to be used as future reference should the need arise. Not surprisingly very few of the other Holkham tenants wrote more letters than they absolutely had to.

1817 saw a slight cooling of enthusiasm. In February a request from Blaikie to FitzRoy to send a waggon and a team of horses to Holkham to collect some trees to be planted at Kempstone, [Letter 17] annoyed FitzRoy who, very busy claying, repairing the new sunk fences and carting stones for the Garden Wall, bricks and lime etc., had no time to spare. "I should have sent a light green cart over with a Mule without taking horses from my farm where this *particular year* they cannot be spared." He wrote firmly. [Letter 18].

Blaikie then got out his heavy gun: "......I trust you will pardon my importunity when I state, That imperious *Duty* calls upon me to request the favor of you to send a team of horses with A Waggon to this place [Holkham] where they will be taken care of, on Wednesday evening the 19th inst. to load the following morning and return to Kempston that evening with the trees. I am certain you will not wish me to call upon any of Mr Cokes tenants to do their *two days* annual duty, upon land partially in *your* occupation......This letter will be conveyed by Mr Banks to Tittleshall who will forward it to you by special messenger, I hope it will be convenient for you to return me an answer by the same conveyance and say whether you can (without any very materiel inconvenience to yourself) oblige Mr Coke by sending your Waggon according to my request. It will be necessary I should be informed of this, as Mr Coke's business must not be neglected, & in the event of its being inconvenient for you to send, I must provide another conveyance."

FitzRoy responded by saying he would send a waggon at "a very great inconvenience" and it is in this letter [Letter 20] that he explains how he was "......not to be considered in the light of Common Tennant, indeed I would not have taken the place under such circumstance, the right of shooting was given me - and I was exempted from doing the days carting works that other Tenants do......6000£ I laid out upon this House only....."

***

In all there are 121 letters to, from, or concerning FitzRoy recorded in the Holkham letter books, and these are only a selection of the total FitzRoy wrote and received post 1816. There are also gaps, years in which no letters were recorded, 1821, 1829, 1830 and 1832. To quote from them in turn would be tedious, and confusing. It is better to approach their contents under headings the Rent, the Lease, his relations with Blaikie (and later Baker), his relations with Coke, with his neighbours, his farm employees, bailiffs etc, servants, social life and family. The letters provide the best illustration of FitzRoy's character and complex relationship with Holkham.

The Lease or absence of it has been already established. The question is how did this effect his relationship with the Estate ? The matter of the waggons mentioned in the above letters is a good example.

While in the Holkham Audit Books FitzRoy is entered in the same way as other Tenants for the purposes of taxes and claiming expenses for repairs etc, he apparently did not feel obliged to give up days to work for Coke as the rest of the Tenantry were bound to. Nor could Blaikie command him so to do. (The trees referred to by Blaikie were for the Ozier Carr, that part of Kempstone which Coke held in his own occupation, for growing timber.) The house the FitzRoys lived in is always entered as the Mansion House, unlike any other farm house on the Estate, though some were as large if not larger. The gardens and lawns around it were treated almost as FitzRoy's private lands, the implication being that, if by some misfortune FitzRoy were to give up the farm, the site of the Mansion and gardens could still be his to live in.

The Rent

The customary manner of paying rent was quarterly, at Holkham. FitzRoy was often away for the Midsummer Audit and frequently refers in his letters to "the usual £100 due at this time."

His rent in 1808 and 1809 was £351, these being the last two years of the 21 year lease he had bought from Johnson's Executors. In 1810 the rent rose to £469-5-0, which included £2-2-0 for grass land added to the farm, £2-0-0 for a newly built cottage, and 10% interest on the £300 it had cost to build the Bailiff's Cottage. The following year improvements to the Bailiff's Cottage increased the rent further to £485-7-0, the extra £14 was 10% on the £140 improvement. In 1812 FitzRoy bought a lifehold interest on the new Cottage (in order to have a vote) and the rent decreased by £2 to £485-7-0; the lifehold rent cost him 6 shillings a year which continued without change until his death.

By 1814 land was added to the farm as the result of the

49

Kempstone enclosure, increasing the rent by £15-0-6 to £498-7-6. The rent remained at this amount for the remainder of FitzRoy's tenure, with the addition of a further £15 a year from 1818, - 7½ % of the £200 it cost to build the Garden Wall. Throughout the period that FitzRoy lived at Kempstone he paid a further £5-0-0 a year as rent to Coke's Private Estate (entailed) for 4 acres of land in Kempstone, late Raven's, and in 1836 another £20 for the last two years of his life, when more land was added to his farm from the Private Estate. During the agricultural depression in 1821 and 1822 FitzRoy was allowed a reduction of £51-6-6 and £80-0-0 respectively.

There is no recorded correspondence between Kempstone and Holkham for the year 1821 and therefore nothing about the rent reduction FitzRoy was allowed that year: possibly he was abroad, for his very strong views on the subject of what constituted a fair reduction are set out in no uncertain terms in the 1822 and 1823 Letter Books. Blaikie's meticulous answers to FitzRoy's grievances illustrate well his desire that FitzRoy should appreciate the thinking behind Coke's policies. They are written without any condescension but with care that FitzRoy should perfectly understand; they are also good examples of Blaikie's scrupulous attention to duty.

**

Letter 54. Blaikie to General FitzRoy 5th Jan.1822

Honble. Sir/ I have received your letter [missing from the Letter Book] of this morning's date, in answer thereto I beg leave to observe *That no circular of the nature you mention has been issued from this Office* - If there had; you would undoubtedly have received a Copy - The information (as to the fact) which you have received (from what quarter I am at a loss to conjecture) is so far correct - That notwithstanding the extreme inconvenience with which the measure will be attended to Mr Coke; He has made arrangements, for making liberal returns to such of His Tenantry who occupy under certain circumstances - *On their paying in full at the Audit next week, the balances of Rent due to him at Michaelmas last,* but not otherwise,

And I have the pleasure of informing you that your name is on that list-

As Mr Coke is now at dinner I shall have no chance of seeing him either this evening or early tomorrow morning, consequently shall not have an opportunity of laying your letter before Him and of receiving his answer to your Query as to the specific sum of money which will be returned to you on your payment in full at the Audit - But you may rely on the accuracy of the information I have given you as to your name being inserted in the list for Returns, and I will add, That it was so placed by Mr Coke's order. I am Honble. Sir, yours etc.ect. Fb.B.

***

Letter 55 FitzRoy to Blaikie 26th July 1822

My Dear Blaikie/ I wrote to you just before I left London, I told you I should be home by the 11th or 12th I got here on Friday Eve the 12th and have been extremely ill with a Billious fever which has prevented my writing to you sooner, I am now only suffering from weakness, having undergone severe discipline from bleeding and dosing.

As I before stated to you my wish to do everything that is proper and just towards Mr Coke, and I trust no one can say I have not done so here in every respect, but the times are such and the difficulties of getting monies due to me paid, I cannot possibly go on as I stated in a former letter without some deduction of Rent, I ask no more than what is just and fair, and what is done to others. Every Landlord throughout the Kingdom are lowering their Rents I have lowered mine 30 per Cent on one Estate and 25 per Cent on another, and also 25 per Cent on Tithe, should times improve I wd. immediately return to my old Rent, and shd. feel bound again to return Mr Coke his old Rent, but for the time being there is no going on at the present price of things at the present Rent - ....Yours Wm. FR.

***

Letter 56 Blaikie to FitzRoy 28th July 1822

Honble. Sir/ I acknowledge the receipt of your letter with its enclosure your check for £100......In regard to the reduction of rent upon your farm, I think I might venture to say, Mr Coke will act in the same liberal manner to you as to his other Tenantry, in so far as relates to the rent at large; You of course do not anticipate a reduction upon the per Centage of money expended by Mr Coke at your request in the building of the Garden Wall, the Bailiff's House and such other buildings as are not necessary for the occupations of the land. The Reductions you mention to have been made to your Tenants are no doubt Liberal and proper. Indeed Landlords must endeavour to meet the times by every means in their power. But no general rule of reduction can be equitable if done by an uniform per Centage, all depends on the original Letting and Local circumstances and it is possible nay very probable that one Landlord may Reduce his Rents 90 per Cent, while his neighbour does not reduce more than 20 per Cent, and the former be the less Liberal Landlord of the two, although the world may extol him as a perfect prodigy of Liberality. The same argument holds good in regard to particular cases upon the same Estate. You are well aware that it is an extreme difficult matter to make an equitable arrangement in such an intricate concern, certainly it is impossible to give satisfaction to every one, and for this very cogent reason, *every man becomes a judge in his own cause*, and in such cases, it rarely happens that men view both sides of the question with perfect impartiality. It is not the nature of man to do so, nor is it to be expected of Him - This failing is carried to such an excess that it is quite common when an occupier has (what is called) *farmed the Landlord,* and brought it into a complete state of dilapidation and in consequence necessitated to resign his occupation. He still believes that he has made some beneficial improvements upon the Estate, and makes application to the landlord for remuneration accordingly, although an impartial man would adjudge the Landlord for a large sum of dilapidation, The mistake originates from the fatal error, in considering *all alterations to be beneficial improvements.* But this is human frailty, and we are taught to bear with one anothers infirmities. I have great cause to regret I was not born and bred a philosopher for situated as I now am, *owing to the ministeriel mismangement of national affairs*, I am in a fair way of being driven distracted. But while I retain my proper senses I shall be proud to subscribe myself Honble. Sir Yrs. etc.ect. F.B.

***

52

Letter 60 Blaikie to FitzRoy 14th January 1823.

Honble. Sir/Be pleased to accept of my humble yet hearty thanks for your remittance of £396-16-4.......You say you are "an excellent Tenant" and I must acknowledge you are so, But what is of very materiel consequence, Mr Coke proves to you, that *He thinks* you are a good Tenant, for He makes you the Liberal sum of *£80* upon your last years Rent........I am Honble. Sir etc. F.B.

***

Letter 61 FitzRoy to Blaikie 15th January 1823 Wednesday evening.

My dear Blaikie/ I only this Eve received your letter.....tho' I am grateful and gladly accept *any reduction* I honestly confess to *you* I expected at *least* 25 per Cent would be thrown off I scarce know of an instance where so little as 15 per Cent has been thrown off by any Landlord. The Duke of Grafton returned to his Tenantry 30 per Cent, the Duke of Portland 50 per Cent, Lord Wodehouse 23 per Cent last year, and this year more, at Litcham. The whole of my Corn sold for £379-16-6 last year, The Labour only was £458-19-9. I pay £40 again for the Bailiffs House and Well (which Well is due) and 7½ per Cent for the Garden Wall, all the Rent is for Land, I can assure you that I am with the Return now minus my Rent. However I must be content with neighbour's Fare, and the same that the other Tenants get, I really think I do not expect too much when I say 30 per Cent wd. be ye least that could be, as ought to be deducted from my rent, and I defy any Farmer to pay the rent even at that deduction on *this Farm* - I do not say this with the voice of anger or complaint, but certainly of disappointment, at the same time as I before said, I am *grateful* for any reduction conceiving Mr Coke is acting by me *the same* as by the *other Tenants*. The Rector of Beeston threw off 30 per Cent on his Tythes - £400 per Ann. would be a good Rent for this Farm, for a good Tenant who paid his Rent to the day and kept the Farm up as I do.......Believe me my dear Blaikie yours etc.etc. Wm. F.R.

***

Letter 62 Blaikie to FitzRoy 17th January 1823.

Honble. Sir/ I have received your letter and I must say I am not a little disappointed that you are not perfectly satisfied with Mr Coke's liberal reduction of the sum of *£80* on your years' Rent to Michaelmas last. I do think it is not correct to argue upon what other Landlords and Tithe holders have done in the way of reduction, many of those who are now cried up as *Liberal* Landlords were never before heard of under that Character - It is well known that if many Landlords were to reduce their rents 50 per Cent, their land would not then let so low (all circumstances considered) as a great part of Mr Coke's Estate - Neither would it have been an equitable adjustment if Mr Coke's abatement of rents had all been on the same scale of per Centage for if that rule had been followed throughout your proportion would assuredly have fallen far short of the sum which Mr Coke returned to you.

You Honble. Sir will probably be not a little surprised when I inform you that a great many (not less than thirty) of Mr Coke's Tenants paid their Rents *in full* at the last Audit and had no return made; and what is more, none asked for, because none could conscienciously be required. It is true in a few instances Mr Coke made returns to the amount of 30, 35 and 40 per Cent, but those were particular, where the Tenants occupy under valuations higher than is customary upon Mr Cokes' Estate and when the crop had been injured to a considerable extent by the depredations of Game, and as well subject to the depredations of the *Parson* - Thus you see, the reductions have not, (as they ought not) been made upon uniform per Centage - And I will add, Mr Coke has made no distinction in that respect between his Tenants *bound by lease to a fine payment* and those who occupy at Will. According to my judgement Mr Coke has in his Abatement of Rents acted with strict impartiallity, by no means pressing those who could pay more than those could not. And I have great pleasure in saying that the principle seemed to be fully estimated by the Tenantry, and that all who received returns from the Audit Table, whether more or less per Centage, seemed to receive the amount with gratitude and perfect satisfaction..........Mr Coke, Lady Anne and Infant, Lady Anson and Family are all quite well - Mr William Coke is now here, I am told he is in good health, but I have not seen him. I am Honble. Sir yours etc. etc. F.B.

This last is one of the most explicit letters Blaikie wrote to FitzRoy. He went to great pains to explain the situation, perhaps in anticipation that FitzRoy would pass it on to his noble friends. But he was also keen for FitzRoy to grasp the fairness of his treatment and to emphasise the state of good relations between them he un-characteristcally added the friendly family news at the end of the letter.

In fact the matter of rent reductions in view "of the depression in the times" on the Holkham Estate depended very much on the date of the Tenant's lease, i.e. when their rents had been fixed; if they were on the last years of a long lease they might hope to survive relatively easily and without help, but any tenant whose lease dated from c.1812, when rents had risen to a far higher amount, would find it more difficult. John Turner took an 18 year lease on a Castle Acre farm in 1818 at an enormously increased rent from that paid by his predecessor: by 1822 he was in deep trouble and was allowed a 35% (£300) reduction. FitzRoy, with no lease and no substantial increase in rent, was fortunate, if not privileged, to be granted any rebate.

The Lease

Holkham leases went from Michaelmas to Michaelmas, when (usually the 11th of October) tenants were expected to hand in their rent, together with bills for money spent on repairs during the previous twelve months, or "Disbursments". In 1836 Baker, Blaikie's successor, describes a visit to Tittleshall "for the purpose of taking in and allowing several Tenants in that district, their Disbursments." [Letter 120]. From the start FitzRoy was treated as the other tenants were when it came to the Estate paying for repairs.

Before Blaikie arrived at Holkham in 1816 and standardised the leases, they had contained several variations mainly to do with crop rotation The four course was not firmly established pre-Blaikie [R.A.C.Parker, *Coke of Norfolk* OUP 1975] although some tenants were practising it e.g. FitzRoy's neighbour Beck of West Lexham who had advised FitzRoy in 1816 to follow his example "as the best suited to my farm." [Letter 12]. The terms of the lease set out all rights of timber, furze, bushes etc. to Coke or his steward, also quarries, minerals, brick earth, chalk, clay, gravel, sand and stones. The landlord had the right to plant trees and set quicks, sow furze seed, to hawk, hunt, fish, fowl, shoot, course and sport over the land. All of these were waived for FitzRoy in 1808. He made roads and planted trees to his own design, though there was some consultation with Coke, [Letter 26] and Blaikie was certainly full of advice on tree planting [Letter 10]. The rights to shoot etc. have already been established. Normally tenants were obliged to keep and maintain at all times gratis one couple of hounds, one greyhound, pointer or spaniel and one game cock for use by Coke. Further the tenant had a duty to protect and preserve all game (except Rabbits), and to prosecute poachers, expenses for this to be paid by Coke.

Tenants were required to pay all parochial and Parliamentary taxes, except for the Land Tax. Along with the others, FitzRoy's land tax was always paid by Coke, the rightful owner of the farm; in 1809 it was £16-06-00 a year, by 1837 it had risen only slightly to £18-06-00. The unpopular Property Tax, which Coke also paid for Kempstone, was £33-17-02 in 1809 and £34-07-04 in its last year, 1820. This tax was much opposed by Coke; FitzRoy attended meetings in Norwich about it in support of Coke; as a landlord himself it was in his own interest.

The house and farm premises were to be kept in good repair and no sub-letting was allowed. The house was to be painted at least twice during the lease, and to be left in good order at the end, no fixtures and fittings to be removed without written consent. It is this clause in the lease which we have to thank for the detailed description of Kempstone Lodge in 1816. When he eventually got his lease a condition was that FitzRoy should insure all the buildings for £5,000.

There were a great many rules and regulations about the care of hedges, ditches and trees, and the penalties included £20 for each and every timber tree that might be damaged. Detailed instructions were given on the four course system (Blaikie guarding against any excuse).

The punctual payment of rent ensured that peaceful and quiet enjoyment was the Tenant's right, but if rent was unpaid for 40 days, or if the Tenant wished to leave, became bankrupt, insolvent, or absconded then Coke had the right to evict the Tenant and claim any rent owing.

The rather ambiguous position that FitzRoy occupied with reference to his obligations is shown by two letters written in August 1818. In the first FitzRoy asks Blaikie for some paint, saying that he has painted the Lodge at his own expense every third year and most of the farm buildings too. Blaikie replies that: ".......Mr Coke does not covenant to find Paint for repairs, on the contrary, all His Tenants engage to paint *twice* in the course of a 21 years lease, and *that at their own cost and charge* - The lease is explicit, nor can I in any way deviate from it, unless by special order from Mr Coke, and I am sure you would not wish me to trouble Him with such a trifling matter......." [Letter 37].

The second, the example of Carriage work which FitzRoy refused to comply with in 1817, [Letter 20] usually involved the tenant in 2 or 3 days work going to Holkham and back, seed and harvest time excepted. When FitzRoy's lease was finally drawn up in 1825, he was asked to do 5 days work with a waggon or two carts, five or six horses and 2 men. Further he was asked (if required) to deliver to the stables at Holkham 2 full waggon-loads of good winter corn straw at the rate of 10/- per load to be paid by Coke. These demands for carriage were standard practice.

But it would appear that, in 1817, Blaikie was not altogether sure how far he could push FitzRoy on the subject; his authority when dealing with the rest of the tenantry was absolute and as FitzRoy's agreement with Coke actually appeared to fit that of a "common" tenant rather more than an "uncommon" one on most matters, it was reasonable to expect he might comply with the carriage rules. Whether FitzRoy did so is unrecorded, but one suspects not, for in 1826 [Letter 81], when the lease was drawn up though not yet signed, Blaikie, while in fact encouraging FitzRoy to collect some reed for thatching which is ready and waiting for him at Holkham, cannot resist giving him a lesson on the subject of efficient carting:

Letter 81. Blaikie to FitzRoy   27th Jan 1826.
".......This weather would be a favourable opportunity for removing the Reed from this place. Mr Abbott [of the Wicken Farm, Castle Acre, a young man FitzRoy liked] is taking advantage of it. He has already

carried four loads and comes for two more tomorrow, He sends his Horses and Waggons off from Castleacre about One in the morning, they arrive here about seven, Stop for two hours, bait [feed] and clean the Horses, they bring their Corn with them and we find them Hay and baiting [food] for the Men. In the mean time our Reed Cutters (being accustomed to the business) load the Waggons *properly*, the Teams start on their return about Eleven, and arrive at Castleacre about six in the evening. We have a presence of Reed in store, and if you are desirous of having some for your repairs, I have no doubt we can supply you with a sufficient quantity for that purpose And as the distance to Kempstone is nearly the same as to Castleacre, I think you cannot do better than follow Mr Abbotts example in the arrangement as I have before stated -- The Reed should be put under cover until it is wanted for use, Mr Abbott puts his in one of his Barns If you cannot spare any part of your Barn for that purpose, You probably can put the Reed into one of your Sheds, or under your Waggon Lodge. You should send two Waggons at a time so that in case of accident, the men assist each other and you should send two *good Ropes* to *each Waggon*, as the Reed requires to be well bound - You should give me previous notice of the first time you intend to send, so that I may the Reed Leaders ready on the spot, and thereby prevent disappointment or delay. Your Team Men should be authorized to fix a time with the Reed loading when they will come for their several loads. The Reed stacks are at the Carpenters Yard near the Hall, and there your Waggons should be placed when they arrive, and the Horses taken to the Hall Stables on the opposite side of the Lake. [1]

I have been most particular in mentioning those circumstances as I should be extremely sorry any mistake or disappointment should occur on so long a journey - The Men will have no pretext whatever for stopping at any Pot House on the Road [2]: they will be well

[1] The arrangement today is exactly the opposite, the Stables which now house the Bygones Exhibition are close to the Hall.
[2] The road from Fakenham to Holkham has no Pot house or pub on it and is always known as the Dry Road.

baited here and if they are promised a Horn of Ale when they arrive safe and in due time at Kempstone they will go home with light hearts - These Pot Houses are great pests and are the principle cause of the accidents which so frequently happen to Team Men and Team Horses, I some years ago in the Winter Season saw a fine Team of yours standing perishing at a Pot House on Brisely Common, and I was so situated at the time I could not go to rout the Man out of the House, the Team probably stood there some hours. I am Honble Sir yours etc. F. B."

***

The first recorded reference to FitzRoy showing an interest in wanting a regular lease comes in Letter 38 which Blaikie wrote to FitzRoy on 5th August 1819: "...With respect to your Lease as from the Tenor of your letter, I am led to believe you misunderstood the nature of such contracts upon this Estate. I will therefore endeavour to explain to you upon paper what I think I must have mentioned to you verbally - It is certainly in Mr Cokes power (and I believe it to be His intention, if you so wish it) to continue the Farm and Premises at Kempston in your occupation at the present rent while he lives. But it is my duty to inform you that it is not in Mr Cokes power to grant you a lease of 21 Years (calculating from the present time) - otherwise than at a yearly rent, equal to the actual Value of the Farm and Premises at the time of granting the said Lease - The stipulations in Lord Leicesters Will are imperitive in this respect - But it is in Mr Cokes power to grant you a Lease for the remainder of the term of 21 years calculating from Mich. 1809. and this has been recently done in regard to Chamberlayne and others......."

***

It may be presumed, since his letter was not recorded, that FitzRoy was asking for a 21 year lease to start right away. Chamberlaine, who farmed the adjoining Manor Farm in Kempstone, had been given a 21 year lease in 1788; this expired in 1809, but in 1818 his son, who had taken over the farm the year before, was given a 12 year lease (a 21 year lease backdated). FitzRoy evidently rejected the idea of only 12 year lease in 1788; this expired in 1809, but in 1818 his son, who had taken over the farm the year before, was given a 12 year lease (a 21 year lease backdated). FitzRoy evidently rejected the idea of only 12 years and persisted in asking for 21, for Blaikie wrote to him again on 16th August 1819:

".....Having discharged the duty of my office in informing you that your proposed extention of the lease beyond the term of 21 years commencing Michaelmas 1809 will not be valid in law - and having subsequently received your voluminous correspondence on the subject, the purpose of which is, expressing an anxious desire on your part to have your lease made out for 21 years commencing from Michaelmas in the present year - I have communicated the same to Mr Coke, and am directed by Him to inform you that He will comply with your request as far as lies in His power - *You being aware that His signature will not make the transaction more legal...*"

***

It appears FitzRoy persuaded Blaikie, for on 21st August 1819 he wrote to him from Quidenham, home of Lord Albemarle where Coke was also a guest, stating his satisfaction at the prospect of a lease. [Letter 41]. However Blaikie won the campaign, for the lease was not granted and nor was it mentioned again until March 1826, nearly six years later, when FitzRoy wrote:

"My Dear Blaikie/ I trouble you with this letter on the subject of my lease which had been so often promised me. It is right I should have it according to the agreement with Mr Coke and myself some years before you came to Holkham and which Mr Coke told me it was my own fault I had not had it sooner....."

Blaikie consulted Coke and answered FitzRoy's request two days later, pouring out conditions, advice and commands in a positive torrent of impatience if not exasperation, most noticeably in the last paragraph:

"Honble. Sir/ I have received your letter of the 2nd Instant and have laid it before Mr Coke, who has directed me to say in answer "If it is your wish Mr Coke will grant you a lease for 19 years from Michaelmas last, that would be to the Michaelmas after his Son will come of Age, if it pleases God to spare his life". As to what you formerly talk of "a running lease for 21 years renewable every year" I have repeatedly said it is quite impossible for such a lease to be *Legal* upon an entailed Estate, and I cannot conscientiously be concerned in preparing such a lease, without previously advising the parties of the risks they run. Such a transaction would be a complete deception and in fact no binding lease to either party - I believe you may have a legal lease for the term above specified, but not longer - Taking it for granted you will feel satisfied with that term. Before I can give proper instructions for preparing said lease, I must request the favor of you, to furnish me with particular information on various matters, with which I am at present but partially acquainted - But before I state those, I humbly beg leave to mention some circumstances which I take the liberty of saying will be well for you to consider, before you determine upon your lease being prepared at the present time.

The present aspect of public affairs is most unpromising. The great probability that the contracting of the circulating medium by the suppression of small country notes, and eventually of those of the Bank of England will make matters still worse. The Revision of the Corn Laws staring us in the face and the great probability of that measure being carried into effect at no distant period, for if the Free Trade system is to be preserved in, *upon a broad basis*, it is quite evident Our Manufacturers cannot compete with Foreigners, unless they can eat bread at nearly as Cheap a rate - Your Lease will be expensive it will cost you upwards of Forty Pounds - The stamp alone will come to about *£30* and those must be paid in the first instance by the Solicitor who prepares the lease - So that it will not answer to have the Lease made, and remain in abayance, to be executed or not, according to the chain of events, for you would have to pay for the lease as soon as prepared whether is was ever executed or not. I mention the latter circumstances to prevent future misunderstanding on that subject, for the Solicitor cannot and will not lay out of his Money, as after paying stamps, and Clerks for Rough Copy and Engrossing together with parchment, little or no profit remains to the poor Lawyer --

It will therefore be necessary, if you Sir, determine upon having your Lease prepared, that you will at the same time inform me of the precise time when you could wish to have it executed - You may calculate upon Mr Coke being at this place immediately after the conclusion of the present Session of Parliament and that He probably will remain here the remainder of the Summer, so that you may suit your own convenience as to time. But whether you determine upon your having your lease prepared now, or at any future period, there will be no harm in your informing me on the following particulars, as those may be acted upon when you think proper -

We have no recent survey of your farm in this Office, and your Farm has greatly altered since the last survey was taken. According to our Estimate the Extent of land you occupy under Mr Coke is 416 acres, including Arable, Permanent Pasture, Mowing Meadow and Plantations within the Farm, I wish you to inform as near as you can calculate.

How many Acres Mowing Meadow including fences? How many permanent pasture do? [ditto] - How many Plantations, Gardens, Scite of Buildings and the residue we will denominate Arable - I hope you will be as exact as circumstances will permit in answering those questions - As it is necessary the quantities of each should be expressed in the lease. Your Rent is stated at £518-7-6 which as I understand it, includes the Mansion House, Offices and Gardens, Stewards House and Farm Buildings, and the lodge Cottage to the Litcham approach and all other accommodation building on the Farm, if there are any Labourers Cottages you will mention them and their inhabitants, *exclusive of your Lifehold Cottage at 6/- a Year reserved rent, which is not necessary to include in the Lease* 416 Acres of Land, more or less, with the Rectorial Tithe on the same, excepting as to Plantations, together with the Rectorial Tithes on other lands in Kempston, exclusive of the Lands in Messr. Chamberlayne and Leeds occupation. You will mention the Names of the occupiers in Kempston who pay Tithes, or Composition for Tithes to you, their names shall be inserted in the Lease - Your Cultivation of the Arable Land, is I believe on the Customary four course shift - In leases on that Course, we usually insert a clause to improve the Tenant, if he should find it convenient to let seeds lay *two* years He may on breaking up, take two successive Crops of Corn. One of which being

Peas or Beans, All other Covenants will be according to the Custom and Usage on this Estate.

I hope that You, Honble Sir, will be explicit in answering the remarks in this letter, so as to occupy as little of my time as possible in further explanation on the subject - The length of this letter, similar to others I am in the constant habit of writing upon similar subjects, and immense number of others upon various matters of official business, and those added to personal execution in directing the complicated Machinery in the Household, the Parish, the Domain and the Estate generally will prove to you in giving this such a consideration, that any situation here is not exactly a sinecure. I therefore pray of You Sir to consider my case, and to have mercy upon me, and not lay a heavier burden upon me than I can bear, I will with pleasure endeavour to discharge the duty I owe to Mr Coke, to his Friends, and Tenantry, but as to giving satisfaction to all, that is quite out of the question. They must however take the will for the Deed, and excuse the imperfections of human nature, from which I am well aware I am not exempt. All I ask is compassionate forbearance, and not to push me down with a load heavier than I can bear - And again praying your Mercy, I subscribe myself

Honble. Sir Your very humble servant F. B.

Poor Blaikie. But the letter had its effect; for although FitzRoy replied by return of post, he restricted himself to just a few lines, but then rather spoilt his good intentions ("I cannot compress all you require in a *Nut Shell*") by adding a repetitious postscript.

But once again no lease was drawn up: the written promise appears to have been enough for although there are a number of letters in 1826 and 1827, it was not mentioned again until March 1828. FitzRoy was now 55 and he had been at Kempstone for twenty years. His dear landlord Coke was 74. Possibly FitzRoy never quite believed Blaikie on the subject of the running lease being invalid and had felt safe enough, but now the twenty-one year mark was approaching and with it a certain apprehension, because of the complications involved. FitzRoy was able to rebuke Blaikie for his slowness, which he did in letter 95 written on 7th March 1828. In it he describes the extent of his farm, repeats once again how he would never have taken "the original offer and promise, had I had any Idea it would not be valid and I certainly would not have laid out what I have done here on the Buildings." The cat and mouse game that he and Blaikie played is given a new boost when FitzRoy mentions his old neighbour, Leeds, "still alive but in a very precarious state." Leeds had a small holding of ten acres, land which FitzRoy had been promised on Leeds's death, and Blaikie jumps upon this to ask does FitzRoy want a lease now, or to wait until Leeds dies ?

FitzRoy replies [Letter 97] that Leeds's land "is an object to this place and to this place only.....I should certainly like to have my lease as soon as convenient, I am, and have been *constantly* improving here [a requirement for all tenants, written into their leases] and I conceive if a lease is necessary for A,B,C,D, or E it is equally so for F. It certainly would be fortunate (as poor old Leeds cannot live long) if he was to die before the lease is made out, as his occupation could be included therein."

***

The next letter [Letter 98] is dated 20 August 1828 and yet again it is from FitzRoy agitating for his lease: "....I must confess when I reflect on your acknowledged punctuality and dispatch of business, I am at loss to guess why I alone amongst Mr Coke's Tenants should be without a lease. The long delay and suspense vexes me." The issue of Leeds's ten acres no longer is one: "by the by He seems to have taken a new lease of his life for He is very hearty and well." FitzRoy, no doubt a little embarrassed, denied he was waiting for Leeds to die, or move, "....I wish by no means to wait for my lease during that period, and trust you will be so good as to comply with my wishes, and I hope it will be ready by Michaelmas 1828 which will save me the disagreeable necessity of again troubling you on this oft repeated subject."

***

Blaikie, seeking to justify himself, replied on 23 August 1828 [Letter 99] and quotes FitzRoy back at himself, giving FitzRoy to understand that he, Blaikie, believed FitzRoy *was* waiting for Leeds to die. This was more than a little unfair.

Francis Blaikie, artist unknown
(By kind permission of the Earl of Leicester)

FitzRoy replied on 26 August 1828 [Letter 100] "........I am really grieved to think you misunderstood my letter, when you imagine I meant to attribute blame to you for not having my lease prepared I can assure you that was not my intention - Allow me to return you my thanks for your civility to me at all times, and believe me with great regard and esteem most faithfully your William FitzRoy." There was, after all, no point in antagonizing the man. Ultimately, no matter what FitzRoy's feelings were, Blaikie was essentially a servant and to servants one should always be polite.

Two days later 28 August 1828 [Letter 102] Blaikie wrote to Stokes, the lawyer at Fakenham, with instructions for him to prepare the lease. In this, [Letter 102] Blaikie allowed himself a criticism, a rare example, no doubt his feelings were a little hurt. "....this lease has been a long time in abeyance as you will see by the date. That was owing to the General's Whims and Fancies, at one time he would have a Lease, at another he would not. He at last seems to have made up his mind on the subject, and is at present eager to have his lease signed by Michaelmas next. You will send your Bill with the lease, and I will present it on the lease being executed. The General is not very punctual in his payments." Ouch.

Mr Stokes's bill was £28.

***

The lease was ready and waiting at Holkham on Michaelmas Day 1828, but FitzRoy did not arrive to sign it. That evening Blaikie wrote to him a curt note [Letter 105]; "...you expressed a Wish to have these leases prepared by Michaelmas and they are so, it now rests with you to have these leases executed."

Unaware of his error in not going to Holkham, FitzRoy suggested that as Blaikie was due to hold a Court at Kempstone on 30th October, he should sign the lease then "...if you would kindly bring it with you." [Letter 106]

"......The manner in which you have proposed for executing your lease is not in accordance with the usage of this office," Blaikie replied on 21 October 1828 [Letter 107] "and I am sure you are too much a man of business to think of transmitting a matter of so much importance, out of the usual and customary routine. I have laid your letter before Mr Coke and I am directed by him to say He will have great pleasure in receiving you at this place when it suits your convenience..."

The final recorded letter on this subject [Letter 108] was FitzRoy's reply written on the following day 22 October 1828.

"My dear Blaikie/ I have this day received your letter of the 21st it is possible I may be at Holkham early on Friday morning for a Couple of Hours and I can then Execute the lease. I cannot myself convince there could have been any difficulty to have signed the lease before competent Witnesses in my place.

How frequently Solicitors send leases down by Coach to be signed before competent Witnesses. I have signed Hundreds that way on my own Estate. But it is immaterial to me whether I sign it in one place or another therefore I shall conform to the usage of your office as you wish me to do, but I can't help smiling at the masonic rule. I had it in contemplation to ride over to Holkham to see Mr Coke some morning and as I before said perhaps on Friday. If not I'll take an early opportunity so to do, I should not have waited for an invitation......"

Eventually the lease was signed: it was, as had been agreed, for 19 years backdated to Michaelmas 1825. FitzRoy's rent continued unchanged; only with the death of old Leeds, who hung on until 1835, did it increase when the aforementioned ten acres were added to Kempstone Lodge Farm.

FitzRoy's Relationship with Thomas William Coke

From the small amount of evidence that exists FitzRoy's relationship with Coke, although extremely important, has to remain a little hazy. Coke was his "dear friend and landlord" and he was perhaps something of a father figure, certainly one whom FitzRoy respected and held in awe - "the personal Love and attachment I feel towards him - my respect and admiration of his publick character...." [Letter 14] - but he was also his equal socially belonging, as they both did, to families who had strong political and neighbourly connections.

Few of the illustrious visitors who came to Holkham would have been strangers to FitzRoy. The Duke of Bedford, the Earl of

Albemarle, the Walpoles etc. were all known to him, and of course his own extensive family were also frequent guests. A rare glimpse of Coke's social life in London is recorded in the memoirs of the Hon. Mrs Calvert, a society hostess, whose unpublished Journals 1789 -1822 were edited by Mrs Warrenne Blake in 1911 under the title *An Irish Beauty of the Regency*. Her entry for the 13 June 1815 : "Mr Coke of Norfolk, General FitzRoy (brother to the late Lord Southampton) and married to his cousin (daughter of the present Duke of Grafton) and Mr Grey came here yesterday. Mr Coke seems a very amiable man, and is much liked and respected. General FitzRoy is very pleasant and lively."

From the Letter Books we know that FitzRoy stayed with the Albemarles at Quidenham in the same house party as Coke [Letter 41] and that Lord Albemarle stayed at Kempstone [Letter 21], but it is doubtful that Coke ever did. FitzRoy suggested in Letter 41, 4 December 1816, that a member of the Coke family might reside at Kempstone one day in the future. This never happened. And the nearest that we know FitzRoy came to enhancing Holkham was to supply some cuttings of Irish Ivy from the Church. [Letter 8]. Coke visited Kempstone, both in the course of his duty, riding over the farm with Blaikie [Letter 31] and socially, in January 1822 [Letter 55] when he called on FitzRoy on his return from Quidenham after the Thetford Wool Fair. Coke's visits to Kempstone had probably been quite regular because in 1823 FitzRoy writes to Blaikie ".....I am told my farm is in high order and my sheep are very good, Mr Coke never comes to look at my farm now, I want a little encouragement in these hard times." [Letter 65]. It was a situation that did not improve for by 1828 Coke had not visited Kempstone for a long time, a fact that FitzRoy much laments: "....my landlord never comes to inspect the premises and Improvements." [Letter 95].

After Blaikie's retirement in 1832 some of FitzRoy's letters are addressed to Coke, rather than to Baker, Blaikie's successor. (Baker had been Blaikie's second in command so it was not a question of a stranger taking over.) However, the letters in question are rather impersonal and it is not possible to detect any waning or increase of friendship. The reason for Coke not visiting Kempstone as often as perhaps he had done in the past, could have been due to his age, and to his interest in his new young family. Coke's good opinion of FitzRoy would appear to have remained constant, for in 1835 he agreed to let Weasenham Hall and later the farm to FitzRoy's eldest son, Captain William FitzRoy.

FitzRoy's relationship with Blaikie

FitzRoy and Blaikie never really achieved any easy harmony, though they both tried hard. Ultimately FitzRoy regarded Blaikie as a pedant, which he was, while Blaikie found FitzRoy annoyingly inconsistent. The fact that FitzRoy was frequently away from Kempstone, often at harvest time, returning refreshed and with clear plans of what he wanted to do next, but not always implementing them, irritated Blaikie immensely. FitzRoy enjoyed a freedom, not merely of movement, that Blaikie found irksome. Though, as has been illustrated, FitzRoy demanded every ounce of wit and tact that Blaikie could summon, stretching him to the full, it was in the end a joyless struggle. It was perhaps a relationship that could never work, Blaikie the patient teacher versus FitzRoy the reluctant pupil. What must Blaikie have thought when in March 1827 [Letter 90] FitzRoy wrote to him "....I do not understand the Corn Laws....I live in hopes and shall most probably die in despair." ?

It is perhaps worthwhile showing just one more side of their characters. Of the two FitzRoy was the more compassionate; true he could afford to be, but his constant pleas on behalf of the poor of the parish show Blaikie in a light that is unsympathetic to a modern view. FitzRoy, and Lady Elizabeth, both wrote more than once to Holkham on the need for more cottages for the labourers, and although Coke agreed, none were built. In March 1827 the poverty in the parish, following the agricultural depression, was such that FitzRoy was moved to act [Letter 88]. He reported that "...we are overburdened with poor, we have difficulty in finding employment for them. I have been carting Mould and Borders [sic] on to Pastures and doing my best to employ as many as I can, being desirous to alleviate Chamberlaines as well as myself, a thought has occurred to me....". He suggests that the poor should be allowed to grow potatoes on an

69

acre of land in Kempstone Plantation [a wood], where there was a clearing and a good deal of borage growing. The digging would employ the superfluous hands and provide food for them as well as improving the land by cleaning it and leaving it more level, all at no expense.

Blaikie replies [Letter 89] that he is surprised Kempstone has a superabundance of labourers, Mr Coke is away at present so he cannot comment on FitzRoy's proposal, but "...you will bear in mind that your good vicar would be entitled to a tenth of the Potatoe crop."

Leaving aside the greedy vicar, FitzRoy reaffirms the existence of many poor and says "....they are made more so by want of cottages which has long time been backstated to Mr Coke and *promised* to be built." He adds the poor in Kempstone have no allotment in lieu of Common rights as they do in other Parishes for fuel. [Letter 90]

Blaikie's position at Holkham at this date, 1827, was very strong. He could have encouraged the building of cottages had he wished to, (his grip on the financial affairs on the Estate was far stronger than Coke's) but his stand was to disassociate himself from such matters, in accordance with his general feeling that too many of the tenants put up too many buildings as it was. His opinion of the Poor had been expressed a few years earlier in a letter to Mitchell Forby in 1820 when, ordering asses off Tittleshall Common, so that the whins could grow more strongly (eventually for the poor's own good), he stated "The Poor are seldom capable of judging between right and wrong." i.e. they bring misfortunes on their own heads. A little harsh to say the least.

However, on the subject of the clergy, at any rate the Vicar of Kempstone, FitzRoy and Blaikie were in perfect agreement. The vicar had an agent, a Mr Murrell, who in 1825 challenged FitzRoy on the Tithes that he paid, upping the amount from 2/- an acre to 3/-. "....by stirring the business of the Tythes [he] has set the neighbourhood thinking.... I wish the *bad* Clergy at the Deuce they certainly do not preach up *unanimity, peace* and *concord*, if they do preach it they do not act up to it..." FitzRoy wrote on 9th August 1825 [Letter 77].

Next time he was in the area, Blaikie called on the Vicar and Mr Murrell and reported to FitzRoy "....The Vicar and his Notable Agent have surrendered that point *at disputation*, but I must say they were not very discreet in bringing it forward....I think it incumbent upon every person who has property at stake to keep a sharp eye upon the Church." [Letter 80].

When FitzRoy's plan to help the Poor by allowing them to grow potatoes is threatened by the Vicar asking for tithes he is fairly shocked "....the Vicar, mean as he is, would, even if he knew the labourers cultivated any trifling part of Kempstone bottom for potatoes, be so cruel as to demand tyth thereon. If he were a man of liberality one might ask him the question and secure his not oppressing the Poor, but he is one of those men I wish to have as little communication with as possible....." [Letter 90].

Whether or not this plan was carried out is unknown.

What is known is that after Blaikie retired in 1832, he was bored, "at a loss" is the phrase used by R.A.C.Parker. After wandering on the continent he returned to the country of his birth, Scotland, from where, in 1840, "he wrote a typically gloomy letter predicting future calamities for the agriculture of Britain from free trade and the `awful encroachments of democracy'". [R.A.C.Parker, *Coke of Norfolk*, OUP 1976]. In his bleaker moments he may have even looked back on his sparring partner FitzRoy with some nostalgia.

FitzRoy and his Neighbours

FitzRoy's immediate neighbour on the south side, and fellow Holkham tenant, was first William Chamberlaine, and then his son Thomas. The Chamberlaine family had been at the Manor Farm since 1788 and continued there long after FitzRoy's death until at least 1870. Their lease, already explained on page 26, was a little precarious, and insecurity of lease was therefore something he may have had in common with FitzRoy. The only thing that is certain is that he and FitzRoy were "sadly off for Cottages for our Labourers who belong to the Parish, and Chamberlayne has often begged Me to solicit You [Coke] to build some Cottages for the Parishioners." [Letter 1].

Another tenuous link may have been that he was a relative of FitzRoy's gardener whose name was Chamberlaine Breeze. Otherwise in his letters to Holkham FitzRoy makes no other mention of this neighbour.

To the north at East Lexham Hall lived Col. Frederick Keppel, to whom FitzRoy was connected by marriage, (son of Frederick Keppel, Bishop of Exeter and nephew of 3rd Earl of Albemarle), whose son, Frederick Walpole Keppel, is referred to in FitzRoy's Will as his "beloved good friend". Keppel père, according to FitzRoy's Will, bore a striking resemblance to the Emperor of Russia. [See Appendix 3] FitzRoy named his youngest son Frederick.

Old Mr Beck, who advised him on the four course cropping at the time FitzRoy first came to Kempstone, lived at West Lexham. Mr Beck had four sons, one of whom took over the farm from his father, while another became FitzRoy's Agent. A considerable part of Kempstone Lodge farm bordered Litcham Common and among his neighbours in the parishes of Beeston, Litcham and Kempstone were Mr Raven, Mr Large, Mr Jarret, Mr Powley, old Mr Leeds, Mr John Davey and the Rector of Beeston, the Rev. Dr. Langton, whose glebe land formed part of the eastern boundary. From 1800 to 1840 the Rector of Litcham was the Hon. and Rev. Armine Wodehouse who also had the livings of Barnham, Bixton and Kimberley, with a house in each. [Dr Puddy, *The Short History of Litcham*, 1957].

From 1823 in Castle Acre, across the valley but significant in that most of the parish was also part of the Holkham Estate, John Hudson was at the Lodge Farm and Henry Abbott at the Wicken. FitzRoy, a keen hunting man, got off to a bad start with Hudson in January 1823, when there was a dispute over the use of a bridle gate on Lodge Farm land. Some time later Hudson rode over to Kempstone "...to wait upon FitzRoy and set the misunderstanding to rights." [Letter 62] And by the October in the following year FitzRoy had certainly visited Hudson and Abbott for he asks Blaikie to allow him a wheel pump for his well "....the same as the Tenants have in Castle Acre where the wells are deep." [Letter 71].

FitzRoy and his employees

Outdoors:

FitzRoy, as has already been said, ran his farm with the help of a bailiff right from the time he arrived at Kempstone in 1808. His

The Sheep Shearing at Holkham, artist unknown.

It is likely that FitzRoy and Blaikie are among the spectators in this painting.

(By kind permission of the Earl of Leicester)

account books have not survived, so there is no record of how many farm labourers he employed, a number which anyway would have fluctuated with the seasons. His first bailiff was the dishonest Prentice. He was followed by Jay, who was certainly at Kempstone in 1816. In January 1818 FitzRoy writes of "my Bailiff" but does not give him a name [Letter 26].

In October 1819 Blaikie wrote to Kempstone Lodge Farm addressing his letter to Mr Breese about a complaint Breese has made concerning the well. It is entered in the Holkham Letter Books to "Mr Breese, Bailiff to General FitzRoy." Breese was in fact not the Bailiff but the gardener. In Letter 45, which Breese wrote to Blaikie on 23 October 1819, he refers to "my Kitchen Garden", and in her will FitzRoy's widow leaves £50 to "Chamberlain Breeze, late Gardiner at Kempstone Lodge....in reward for his long and faithful Services." [PCC Will 361 June 1839]. It appears very unusual to employ a gardener as agent in this way, but this is what happened over the following twelve months. There were several letters between Blaikie and Breese, proper letters not just notes. Nor did FitzRoy, who wrote no letters to Blaikie during this period, appear to be away: "...I shall lay your letter before my Master..." wrote Breese to Blaikie [Letter 44]. Nor, again, was he doubling as a Bailiff: "...if it is convenient for him [FitzRoy] to send you or the Bailiff..." Blaikie to Breese [Letter 49].

Whoever was the Bailiff (probably no longer Jay), he left without warning in October 1820, perhaps not caring for the unusual arrangement. Breese informs Blaikie "General FitzRoy being much occupied just now owing to the Bailiff having run away....." [Letter 53]. This letter, about the need to mend barn doors, is the last recorded one from Breese. He stayed on at Kempstone, in 1830 married Charlotte Thompson, [Kempstone Registers] and was almost certainly still there in 1837 at the time of FitzRoy's death.

There are no letters to and from Holkham in 1821, but by 1822 the status quo has been resumed and FitzRoy is writing to Blaikie about the rent. He does not mention anything about a Bailiff.

By 1828 FitzRoy had employed Mr Beck as "my agent". FitzRoy wrote to Blaikie: ".....he shall wait on you at any time you think proper. He is more convenant [sic] in business than I am and will explain more clearly and more concisely than I can. I think when you come here you will be pleased with the state of the farm and premises under Mr Beck's good management." [Letter 95] He sounds fairly new. Beck stayed with FitzRoy until 1836, when he left "for no fault on either side, for in consequence of Mr Becks taking to be an Auctioneer, he cannot of course spare so much of his time as heretofore." [Letter 121].

[Hugh Beck, Auctioneer of Fakenham, told me in August 1994 that the firm had been founded about 150 years ago, but that unfortunately all the archives had been removed at the time of the Prudential takeover in the early 1980's].

The only other named farm employee (1828) is William Shingles, Shepherd. Shingles was shepherd at Kempstone since at least 1813 when it was recorded [*Norwich Mercury* July 1813] that he won a prize at the Norfolk Agricultural Society Show for rearing 312 lambs from 230 Ewes.

Indoors:

FitzRoy employed a Butler called Thomas Buckley, "my upper servant", who lived in a cottage which FitzRoy purchased and was next door to the shepherd's cottage. The Kempstone Church registers record that Thomas Buckley, Butler, and his wife Maria had a daughter Elizabeth christened in 1814; seven more children were born to them by 1827. Thomas Buckley's burial took place at Kempstone in 1835, when he was 63. The same year his widow married one Abraham Lewis.

There are no other records of named servants; in his letters FitzRoy mentions a housekeeper (reporting on the dry rot) [Letter 42] and Lady Elizabeth FitzRoy's will is witnessed by Robert Sewell, Professor of Music, Norwich. But you may rely on there being servants, a lady's maid, nurse and nurse maid for the boys when small, cook, possibly pastry cook, 2 or 3 kitchen maids, still room maids, housemaids, laundress, boot boy, and footmen. Also coachman, groom etc, though sometimes at this period footmen doubled as coachmen and grooms.

FitzRoy's Family and Friends

FitzRoy was close to his family, despite, but perhaps *because* of the large number of brothers and sisters and the ever present grim reaper. Bereavement can draw families closer and FitzRoy had more than his fair share of the uncertainties of life's brief span. While still in his twenties, within a five year period from 1795 to 1800, his younger brother and fellow soldier, Robert, died, also his elder brother Henry, his sister Emily, his sister Susanna and his father. By 1810, after a further spate of funerals, he had lost his mother, his brother George (2nd Lord Southampton), another brother, Warren, and his sister, Louise.

Of the twelve siblings who lived to adulthood and his parents, a family of fourteen, only four were left. [A brother Frederick was born in 1769, but I cannot trace him]. Loss on this scale was not altogether unusual, but that made it no less of a heavy burden for those to whom it happened, and to this toll must also be added his first wife Catherine in 1808.

He was a little more fortunate with his own children, who at any rate all survived infancy. He sent them to Bury St Edmunds Grammar School [Suffolk Green Book XIII], an interesting contrast to Eton where his brothers were, and Harrow where his cousin sent his sons. As their mother, Catherine, left each of them a legacy of c.£5,000, it is doubtful whether money was the reason more likely, as a self confessed under-educated person himself, FitzRoy had more faith in a straight up and down grammar school as a being a sound educational establishment in contrast to the known horrors of an early nineteenth century public school.

The only reference FitzRoy makes to his children in his letters to Holkham is in Letter 20 written on 9 February 1817 when he says his Son was coursing (hares) and he was beating. As today, there were then a great many hares about, to the distress of FitzRoy: ".....I hate them they hurt my fences and in every way injure my Property, eat my Turnips, Corn etc." [Letter 20]

One can imagine he took pride and pleasure in sharing country life with the boys. His affection for his sons, with the exception of Arthur, whom he does not mention, is shown in his will. In it he refers to their mother's settlement money which left them "better off than many poor younger Sons", ever a dreaded fate among the ranks of the landed gentry. ".....God bless them all, I love them dearly, they are good honourable fellows." He was also extremely fond of his "beloved nephew" the 3rd Lord Southampton.

The FitzRoys did a fair amount of visiting. They were generally in London for part of June and July, and were often away during August as well (missing the harvest and the mid-summer audit). Each September was spent at Euston, and on occasion they stayed at another FitzRoy house, Whittlesbury Lodge, Towcester. In 1822 they went to Buxton for a month, for Lady Elizabeth's rheumatism. Another year there was a tour of Wales. Frequent visits to Lord Crewe in Cheshire (a house to which many fashionable and interesting people were invited, including the Rev. Sydney Smith, an exact contemporary, who sadly could not find the time) and to Lord Bagot, FitzRoy's brother in law, in Staffordshire. Lady Elizabeth's brother, Lord Charles FitzRoy, stayed at Kempstone, sometimes in his host's absence. In explaining his own absences to Blaikie FitzRoy uses the phrase "not in the country", though this is more likely to mean not in the *County* rather than abroad. The FitzRoys stayed in several Norfolk houses, including Quidenham and Holkham as has already been mentioned, and from the *Jerningham Letters 1780-1843* edited by Egerton Castle in 1896 it is known that they were guests at Rainham and Costessey. The reason for these last two invitations was their acquaintance with H.R.H. the Duke of Gloucester. The duke was a grandson of George II and in 1816 he married his first cousin, Princess Mary, daughter of George III and erstwhile admirer of FitzRoy's elder brother, Charles. [see page 4] Earlier in the century her sister Princess Amelia had wanted to marry Charles FitzRoy but was prevented from doing so by the Royal Marriage Act passed in 1772, though this had not stopped her believing that they were betrothed and when she died in 1810 she left Charles all she possessed. Not as exciting as it sounds, for in fact she owed *him* several several thousand pounds. Charles FitzRoy was an attractive man, certainly to the two royal sisters: "Princess Mary had also been much in love with this fascinating equerry and jealous of her sister Amelia, and had created a great deal of mischief." [Bernard Falk,

The Royal FitzRoys, Hutchinson, 1950.] Princess Mary's husband, the Duke of Gloucester, whose mother was a Walpole, came to Norfolk for the sport.

It is a little doubtful that FitzRoy had very friendly feelings towards the Duke, for when visiting Mrs Calvert (see above) in 1815 he had given her an account of his brother's and Princess Amelia's attachment, and insisted that the Prince Regent had behaved very ill and cheated his brother and "he abused them all and says they are liars, selfish, and are on no occasion to be depended upon. If his report is true, I am sure it is a lamentable case to have such a Royal Family." [The Hon. Mrs Calvert, *An Irish Beauty of the Regency*, unpublished Journals, 1789 - 1822: edited by Mrs Warrenne Blake, 1911.]

However, in December 1820 the Duke of Gloucester and a party of 20 were staying at Rainham, at that time rented by Colonel Dixon, "The party consisted of his [the Duke's] aide du camp Sir Archibald Murry, Lord and Lady Charles Townsend, General and Lady E. FitzRoy, Colonel Dalton, the Keppel family, Lady Anson and Mr Coke [his daughter] and six Dixons.... they all went to Holkham on Saturday and were to be *32* there." [Young Lady Jerningham to Lady Bedingfield, *The Jerningham Letters 1780-1843* edited by Egerton Castle, Richard Bentley and Co. London 1896 Vol.II] Young Lady Jerningham goes on to say "Lord Charles lives in a *very* small house near and is to come into Possession, in *eleven* years, of Rainham and 15000 a year, at present he has not 2000, Lady Charles was his cousin a Miss Loftus, a very pretty young modest looking person. Cabinets of all sorts and sizes about the house, high backed ivory and ebony chairs, old French commodes running riot all about and several pictures wanting *feeding* dreadfully. There is a Cary amongst de Vere's Captains and a Peyton, You would delight in going over all this, but the *real inhabitants* are wanting, and an Uncle Lord John and the present expectant *quarrel* about every thing to be done; so that this old house is in a pleasant state of ruin, it *was* of the Elizabethan age, but *is* of Inigo Jones. FitzRoy and ourselves I perceived took much more interest than any one else in the whole concern." This agrees with Mrs Calvert's description of FitzRoy: "very pleasant and lively" he had by no means lost his enthusiasm for life.

The following year, in November 1821, it was the lot of the Jerninghams at Costessey to entertain the Duke of Gloucester ("we put off the evil day as long as possible") "His Royal Highness and Captain Foster, his Equery arrived on Tuesday, at 5 o'clock. General and Lady Elizabeth FitzRoy and the Dixon family (the Duke's great friends) having previously arrived. Everything went off extremely well......We killed about 100 Head of Game in two days" wrote Sir G. Jerningham to Lady Bedingfield on 10 November, and the following day Henry Bedingfield wrote to the same recipient ".....The party staying in the house, were General and Lady FitzRoy (she is sister to Lady Blachford and I told her that Lady Blachford had dined with us at Ghent) Col. Dixon and his family who live at Rainham. Other people came to dinner....We are going to meet him [the Duke] again tomorrow at Rainham, and from thence I think I shall go to Narford having an invitation from Mr Fountaine. All the world is to be at Swaffham Coursing Meeting and I feel inclined to add one to the number." [*The Jerningham Letters* ibid.]

FitzRoy was already known to the Jerningham family; they had attended the Prince Regent's Fête in 1811 [see page 13], and when Lady Bedingfield, long resident in the Netherlands, returned to England on the 17 of May 1819, her diary for the following day records: "Dined at General Milner's. Company 2 Princes of Hesse Philipstal, General and Lady Elisabeth FitzRoy, Lord John FitzRoy, Colonel Talbot of the Guards, Colonel and Mrs Doyle." [*The Jerningham Letters* ibid.]

These tantalizing glimpses of FitzRoy at play must suffice. No doubt other accounts exist, but this is enough to confirm that he and Lady Elizabeth, "pleasant and lively", were, like his parents, sociable animals.

***

Lady Elizabeth FitzRoy, his second wife, was assuredly une grande dame. Her refusal to believe her husband's assertion that they were living beyond their means, as he mentions in his will, was probably rooted in the safe knowledge of her own personal fortune. She was, after all, the daughter of a Duke and had not been bought up to budget. She was more given to gestures such as: "Be it remembered that Lady Elizabeth wife of Major General the Hon.William FitzRoy has presented to this Parish a new Bell weighing 4 Cwt. 12r 1lb, cast by Mr William Dobson of Downham, Norfolk and hung 19 December 1820." But money did come into it and a note is added: "Total expence, exclusive of the old Bell in exchange, £20." This is recorded on the flyleaf of a Kempstone Register. In the same year she presented a golden pencil case to Edmund Beck [so says Hugh Beck of Fakenham, August 1994]. These two were doubtless not the only gifts she made. She certainly did not lose her imperious habit of always addressing Blaikie in the third person in the letters she wrote to him over the years.

Both Lady Elizabeth and her husband enjoyed hunting, and to this end bridle gates were installed "for the ladies" but also, one suspects, for FitzRoy whose infirmities would not encourage him to jump too many hedges. There is a record of one at Castle Acre on Hudson's farm [Letter 60] and another on Tittleshall Common installed at Lady Elizabeth's request [Letter 73].

**

A little surpisingly, though not altogether when it is remembered that FitzRoy was a semi-invalid, he owned a large library. After his death among his effects to be sold, [Notice in the *Norfolk Chronicle* October 1837, see Appendix 4], auctioned by one William Beck, were 800 books. Hume's *History of England* in 13 volumes (handsomely bound) and *Vancouver's Voyage round the World* in 6 vols were perhaps acquired with his sons in mind. *Lord Byron's Works* in 9 volumes and the *British Theatre* in 34 volumes, [further proof that he had been a pupil at Newcome's Academy?] besides Walter Scott and 3 volumes of Hogarth's illustrations, were probably not. He also had "a pair of handsome globes, quite perfect." And in addition to the books there were 112 copies of the *Quarterly Review*, one for each quarter of the 28 years he had been at Kempstone. The 800 volumes were left to his wife, and as they were to be sold, may be counted over and above the books she chose to keep.

**

At the time of his death FitzRoy was the last surviving member of his family, his elder sister Charlotte, Lady Dungannon, having died in 1828, his brother Charles in 1831, and his youngest sister, Georgiana Posonsby in 1835. By now he was a grandfather, his eldest son, William, had four sons and his youngest, Frederick Thomas William Coke FitzRoy, one. Both these sons were living in Norfolk. The Kempstone registers record the baptisms of three of William's sons, though the ceremonies had actually taken place at Congham where William lived. The third of these babies, Ferdinand, born 15 June 1833, was baptised by his uncle the Rev. Frederick Thomas William Coke FitzRoy.

Of FitzRoy's other three sons, George William Howe was killed at the Battle of Navarino in 1827, Arthur William Bagot was in the Indian Army and Charles William Henry Gage was in the Navy, and like Nelson had lost an arm.

FitzRoy died aged 64 at Kempstone on 19th May 1837 and was buried there on the 27th. His will [Appendix 3] he must have drawn up himself for it reads like a letter. In it he asked to be buried in Kempstone Church, with a "plain marble Slab like the one for George and Lady Dungannon." The first line of his will: "This is my Will unfortunately I have little or nothing to leave -" confirms his low financial position. The Camden Town property was mortgaged for £3000, he owed the Fakenham Bank £2000, his wife's Trustees £3000 and William Heard, a descendant of the eighteenth century Kempstone farmer, a further £2000. Consequently he directs his executors, his wife and eldest son, to sell all the Kempstone furniture, horses, carriages, farm stock, pictures, plate, linen, china, wine, books etc. in the expectation that it will raise enough money to pay off part of his debts. To his wife he left Gravarin Cottage [whereabouts unknown.] By 1837 he owned four freehold cottages in or near Kempstone, for his sons when they came of age, so that they might have a vote, but makes no mention of this property.

His will contains a quotation which I have not managed to place: "I wish I could leave her [his wife] more, but poor Stevenando raw not so more than he can so I leave...." This must have been a favourite of his for his eldest son William quotes it in a letter to Holkham some years later.

Lady Elizabeth FitzRoy survived her husband by two years, she lived in Gloucestershire for the last few months of life, but her will had been made before she left Kempstone and in it, true to her husband's wish, she left £3,000 to the eldest son William, £4,000 to Frederick, the Rector and the residue "of my paternal Fortune", after several other bequests, to Charles, the third son, who had lost his left arm while serving in the Navy. One of the two witnesses to her will was Robert Sewell, Professor of Music, Norwich.

FitzRoy's Sons

His eldest son William Simon Haughton Clarke became a soldier. He married a Norfolk bride in 1829, Anne Bagge of Stradsett. By 1835 he was a Captain and living at Congham Hall, but later that year became a Holkham tenant when he and his young family moved to Weasenham Hall. Two years on he took over the Hall farm, with the shooting rights over Wellingham, Weasenham and Great Massingham, but only following some protests about the rent, which he considered was rather high. After his father's death William fell out with Coke over the Ostrich public house in Weasenham. The landlord had recently died and William saw this as a good opportunity for closing it down ".....the rendez vous of all the rogues and vagabounds in the neighbourhood, besides in so small a Parish a Publick House is quite unecessary and entirely frustrates the wishes of the occupiers of the land in the Parish to keep their Labourers in a state of re-spectability...." [Holkham Letter Book 1839]. Oh dear !

Happily for the Weasenham parishoners Coke did not agree with him. William then became a J.P. and in 1839 was accused of dealing harshly with Mrs Brunton, the landlord's widow, for it was now in his power to refuse her a licence, which he did. It is here that he quotes "Poor Stephenando cannot do more than he can do." [Holkham Letter Book. ibid.]. Further unrecorded discord arose in 1841, probably on the same subject, for Coke, now Lord Leicester, threatened to take William to law, and there was also talk of William witholding rent. In 1843 the matter was still unresolved with William continuing to refuse Mrs Brunton a license, saying that she kept a disorderly house.

In April 1844 William wrote to Lord Leicester (Thomas William Coke died in 1842 and was succeeded by his eldest son) to say that he had bought a place nearer to London and gave notice of his intention to give up his lease at Michaelmas. His last letter, in January 1845, is addressed to Holkham from Banstead Place, Epsom.

A foot note to this is that the next tenant of Weasenham Hall was William Beck, wine and spirit merchant, and erstwhile auctioneer, who died 1866 and was buried at Mileham.

***

The second son, George, joined the Navy. He was a Lieutenant in 1827 and fought at the Battle of Navarino where he was killed. Blaikie, writing to Lady Elizabeth in December 1827, says: ".....I presume to solicit the favour of your Ladyship, to present my humble and dutiful respects to General FitzRoy and I beg leave to say I in common with this family, and the whole neighbourhood sympathize with your Ladyship and General FitzRoy in the afflicting loss you have recently sustained. It is not in human power to administer a healing balm to your Minds, yet it may be some consolation to be assured your neighbours in particular, and the County in general are sensibly affected on this much lamented occasion." [Letter 93]

***

The third son, Arthur, joined the Indian Army, the Bombay Cavalry. He lived until 1879 according to Burke's Peerage, but does not get a mention in either his father's will or his step-mother's.

***

The fourth son, Charles, another sailor, also saw action, for he lost an arm and at the request of his father, was the chief beneficiary of Lady Elizabeth's will. He married on the 18 May 1837, the day before his father's death. He died in 1886, his wife in 1908.

***

The fifth son, Frederick Thomas William Coke FitzRoy, joined the Church. He married in 1834 Emilia L'Estrange Styleman of Snettisham and was Rector of Ringstead in Norfolk. He inherited property in Highgate (the Grove) in 1851 under the will of his aunt Eliza, widow of the General the Hon. Charles FitzRoy, and died in February 1862. [County Council Survey of London 1936].

Conclusion

Neither of the tenants who followed FitzRoy at Kempstone had trouble in obtaining a long lease. At Michaelmas 1837 a 21 year lease for Kempstone Lodge Farm was granted to James Clegg Moss of Liverpool, at an annual rent of £530, the same that FitzRoy had paid. William FitzRoy jnr. had shown no interest in succeeding his father at Kempstone, nor even of buying the furniture etc, which he described as "very plain indeed, but at the same time for the most part in good Conditions." [Holkham Letter Book, 1837].

At Weasenham Hall William lived with furniture which Coke had purchased from the previous tenant Mr Pearce. Moss stayed at Kempstone until 1850, when William Money Farrer took over, being given a lease for 18 years from 1852 at £630. In the Kempstone Registers Farrer is described as Gentleman Farmer. However, neither of these tenants had need for a Bailiff, in Keary's 1851 report the "Bailiff's house which stands in the yard is now divided into two dwelllings and contains two sitting rooms and four bedrooms." Kempstone Lodge Farm had reverted to the normal Holkham usage.

**

What mark did FitzRoy make on Kempstone Lodge Farm besides gentrifying the house and gardens? His tenancy lasted thirty years, so that a certain amount of change occurred inevitably. After a shaky start, FitzRoy farmed on the four course system: his neighbour had advised him that this method would be best suited to his farm, advice endorsed by Coke. On his arrival at Kempstone he had had his own ideas, which had not always been successful, for he admits "I have seen my Error on Hurrying Alterations which have caused several times going and undoing at Great Expence." [Letter 12].

At the beginning of FitzRoy's tenancy the farm land might indeed have been in need of much "improvement" as FitzRoy always claimed, but the stock was excellent, Mr Johnson's animals won prizes at the Holkham Sheep Shearings and at the Norfolk Agricultural Society Shows [*Norfolk Chronicle: 1803 to 1808*]. Johnson had also been in the vanguard of progress in acquiring a threshing mill described by Arthur Young in his General View of the Agriculture of Norfolk published 1804 as: "one of the best I have seen, if not the very best of the large machines......he [Mr Johnson] attributes the common complaint of their being always out of order, to original errors or inattention in the construction." This comment shows Johnson to have been an attentive and successful farmer, his machine, like his landlord's, was made by Mr Wigful of King's Lynn. In 1800 when Coke bought his, the cost was almost £500. Threshing machines required six to eight horses, six men and one woman according to Arthur Young, and were much cleaner than the flail and much cheaper. John Turner at Castle Acre had one, used in a barn [Holkham Audit Books 1822] and a few years later in 1830 Henry Abbott of the Wicken Farm, also of Castle Acre, wrote to Coke expressing great concern that "the Mob" were close by in South Acre and likely to attack *his* threshing machine at any moment. (They didn't.) [Henry Abbott letter to Coke, in T. W. Coke's personal letter book at Holkham.]

Fitzroy did create water meadows, from what had previously been waste land, a practice much encouraged on the Holkham Estate, but while this increased the acreage of the farm, it also increased the rent. Edward Beck who farmed next door in West Lexham began work on his water meadows in 1804 under the instructions of Mr William Smith who came from London to give him directions at a cost of £45. [Holkham Account Book A/47]. By 1812 Beck had been so successful that his rent was put up by £100, an increase of nearly twenty five per cent as a reward for "improvements by irrigation." [Holkham Audit Book for 1812].

Certainly FitzRoy was an enthusiastic tenant and keen to impress his landlord, money was not stinted when it came to buying stock, seed or implements. The farm was successful, as judged by the

Holkham agent: ".....your whole occupation always is in the highest possible order... admirably well cultivated..." [Holkham Letter Books 1818 and 1819].

***

Keary's 1851 report, fourteen years after FitzRoy's death, says Kempstone Lodge Farm "is well laid out with convenient roads and straight fences, they abound however with young trees which are injurious alike to them and to the crops." (Overhanging trees or too many planted in the hedgerows were considered to be a bad thing as they would draw up the moisture and goodness from the land at the expense of the crops, or in this case, the hedgerows as well). Of the fields he says that the land is either badly drained, or thin and poor, especially where there is a bleak northern aspect, and that much of it would benefit from "a higher system of farming than has hitherto been pursued." [Keary's 1851 Report on all the Holkham farms, Holkham archives] Allowances should be made for the intervening years when standards may have dropped (and expectations rose, Keary is pretty sniffy about the farm buildings and their lay out, most of which were designed and put up by FitzRoy) but a conclusion must be drawn, that while FitzRoy was not unsuccessful, he perhaps lacked the touch of a truly innovative farmer such as John Hudson jnr. of Castle Acre who, as Keary marvelled, produced from inferior land and thin soil "such an enormous bulk of roots and corn [as is] truly astonishing."

He was not, in effect, the Vita Sackville West of the farming world. The state of FitzRoy's finances at his demise was not necessarily due to his failure in making a commercial success of his farm. Without a doubt FitzRoy's lifestyle ate up a large part of his income; he may not have always been prudent, though he tried to be, but he did have fun. Entertaining and being entertained were so much a part of him, and of his class and time; no-one lived life more to the full than he. He was ambitious and enthusiastic; he did not take to farming casually, but gave of his best. Kempstone Lodge Farm was "well laid out with convenient roads and straight fences" [Keary]. Thanks to FitzRoy, the arable land had been "constantly improved", and at his death the stock put up for sale was of the highest quality. [see Appendix 5].

Of his relationship with Holkham, FitzRoy might be judged fortunate in his timing, for he 'caught' Coke in his prime, a younger, or an old Coke, might not have been so ready to enter into such an arrangement with a friend. The risk, if risk there was, which Coke took in letting Kempstone to young FitzRoy in 1808 paid off; he was not let down. And as for FitzRoy, he lived, despite his misgivings of "living in hope and dying in despair", as good a life as any might hope to, certainly no worse.

Hudson of Castle Acre appears on Coke's monument at Holkham, by another accident of date, for he was alive in 1842 when Coke died and lost no time in arranging for the said monument to be erected. [Newspaper cutting Book Holkham archives, unnamed newspaper.] If FitzRoy had lived out his full span of three score years and ten, i.e. till 1843, he would certainly have contributed to the immortalizing of his "dear Landlord" and would he now be remembered by some stone carved bas relief as Hudson is, or taken a more modest role and remained in obscurity as "one of Mr Coke's worst tenants" for so he had described himself, with laughter, in 1815 ?

The End.

Appendix 1.

In 1816 Blaikie was ordered by Coke to take a General View of his Norfolk Estates and to make a Report.

On 8 August 1816 he wrote up his report on Kempstone, which he said was under a promise "of a lease for 21 years commencing 1807."

"Very extensive buildings in good repairs, a Piggery establishment now erecting - Did not see the General, and could not learn whether the Buildings are Insured. They should be for £5,000 - Pays about 3/- in the actual pound Poor Rates and 2/- per Acre - Vicarial Tithes. Cultivated upon a four course shift - in very high order, generally clean. Turnip follows in fair order and are very promising for Crops, much money has been extended in modelling and improving this beautiful farm, some claying still wanted - The Grassland upon this farm is managed in a very superior stile (sic) an experiment of top dressing upon the permanent Grassland now in progress vizt. between Lime, Rape Dust and Folding with Sheep - Sheep are also Folded upon the layer, to be broken up for Wheat - the Fences are managed in a very superior manner, the Plantations thriving, the Roads well laid out and kept in good repair. The general arrangement and management of this fine farm show superior information, and persevering application of the occupier. *Here is much to admire and little to condemn.*
Kempston Church, kept remarkably neat clean etc. the Chancel wall rather dangerous, and the roof wants repairs - The Church is planted round with some Irish and common Ivy is picturesque, but when grown over (as it soon will be) will be damp - *Cuttings of Ivy may be had here for Holkham* - This pretty rural Church is a fine feature on this neat domain, on which superior trust is displayed in the formation and in the admirable nicety and perfect order and cleanliness with which it is maintained - The Kitchen and Fruit Gardens does certainly want a wall to make the place complete - But this would be more the comfort and convenience of the occupier than of any real benefit to the Estate - The Stock generally well selected, some very shabby working Horses."

Appendix 2.

FitzRoy and the Sheep Shearings taken from the *Norwich Mercury* and the *Norfolk Chronicle:*

1807　(While he was still at Great Witchingham): FitzRoy sold 1 0 Southdown Theaves for £47 and an aged sheep with 4lbs 2oz of wool sold for £47.

1808　He entered some Leicester rams and won a prize for a Leicester wether, a silver cup worth 10gns.

1809　No prizes, but he entered a fat Leicester wether carcase 8st 5lb 8oz.

1810　Not there.

1811　No prizes, but he sells there five merino and mixed bred Hoggets at £20 each, 10 Southdown Shearlings at 20½gns and 10 at 23gns. And more Southdown Shearlings for 28gns. The very best price for these was 34gns.

1812　Showed a Southdown Ram.

1813　Did not show any animals, but proposed a toast, Coke's own, at a dinner "Live and Let Live."

1814　Showed a Devon Bull, got a special mention for it.

1815　Showed nothing, but at the dinner on the second day General FitzRoy rose and: "As one of Mr Coke's worst tenants, he said, it might be presumptious in him to put himself forward on this occasion, however, he trusted, with such a good example before his eyes, he would improve, and took occasion to thank Mr Coke in handsome terms for the advantages he had received from his advice and instruction."

1816   FitzRoy's shepherd Wm.Shingles won a prize.

1817   No entries from FitzRoy although he was present.

1818   FitzRoy was away in London this year.

1819   No entries but FitzRoy was present, and his health "was give" at the Tuesday dinner, and he gave testimony to the drill system as practised on his own farm.

1820   No entries, but he was present.

1821   FitzRoy was not there, though he won 1st prize for his best Shearling Southdown Ram.

End of Sheep Shearings.

***

Appendix 3

Will of The Honble. William FitzRoy 1837

This is my last Will unfortunately I have little or nothing to leave --
my Sons are all provided for and will at my death have the 5th share
of the Settlement money [of] their Mothers property minus the Sums
each have already had they will be better off than many poor younger
Sons but be that as it may I wish I had any thing to leave them God
bless them all I love them dearly they are good honourable fellows
To my beloved wife Elizabeth I leave for her life the interest of all
my Personal Property and the residue of the money in Bankers hands
if any left after paying of my debts I conceive the property here at
Kempstone ffurniture Horses Carriages ffarm live and Dead Stock
Crops pictures plate Linnen China Books Wine etc.etc. to be worth
5000£ 2000£ of that goes to ffankenham Bank to pay off a debt woth
2000£ they have for money lent me to go on here for I have kept too
large an establishment to go on without borrowing I have always kept
telling my wife we were living beyond our income but she always
turned a deaf ear to it and I am sure she thought me stingy I would
never convince her to the contrary my own expenditure was very little
my Bankers books if referred to and looked back to will show how
every farthing was spent for all monies went through my Bankers
receipts and payments but as I said before to my wife Elizabeth I
leave the interest of all my personalities [sic] and property here or
elsewhere Camden Town property there is 3000£ Mortgage on that at
4 per cent that must be paid off to pay the Trustees 3000£ the income
from the residue my wife has for her life as I before said as it is
included in and is part of my property at her death it goes to my son
William 1/2 or George's 1/5th share of the Settlement money belongs
to me 3000£ of that goes to Lady E ffitz Roy's Trustees for money
3000£ I borrowed of them the remained after paying Heard 2000£ I
owe them which is but a trifle the interest for my wife's life as she is
to have and at her death it goes to my son William and my
funeral to be as little expensive as it is possible to be where the tree
falls there let it lay I should like to have a plain marble Slab like the
one for George and Lady Dungannon put up in Kempstone Church

wherever I may happen to be buried in preference to where that is Should I not be buried in Kempstone Church I leave to my dearly beloved wife Gravarin Cottage and land for her life & at her death to go to my son William I shld like dear Charley & the others to have some token of my love & affection at my wifes death or sooner if she approves it I shld say

> To Charles my Silver Teapot
> To ffredk. my Silver Coffee pot
> To Wm. my Silver Cocoa pot
> To Lord Southampton my
>   beloved Nephew my silver
> Teapot that was his father's

In short my dear wife will let them have a keepsake from me I have 3 Dukes of Grafton let my sons at my wife's death each have one print of Lord Bagot ffredk. is to have this William to have his mother's picture by Hopner Charles the miniature by Mrs Moe and all the Sailors Lord Howe Sir S Smyth Lord Nelson (one of them) Lord H Seymour print of TW Coke and the old D. of Grafton and King Charles Wm. to have them at my wifes death In short Wm to have every thing at my wifes death not mentioned for his brothers God bless my dear wife my heart is too full to say more I wish I could leave her more but poor Stevanando raw not so more than he can so I leave all I have the power to leave her for her life and at her death to go to my son William Save & except the trifles I have mentioned & I shld like to leave 20£ to Wm. Gray this is my Last Will all former Wills are null and void As witness my hand this 14th day of March 1836.............signed William Fitz Roy Lt.Gen.

I shld like Lord Albemarles print and a print of the Emperor of Russia to be left to my beloved good friend ffredk.Walpole Keppel at my wifes death: the Emperor of Russia we always tht. so like Keppels father I leave my wife Residuary Legate and joint Executrix with my son William as Executor.

Appendix 4.

Norfolk Chronicle October 1837

Important Sale of Furniture

Mr Wm. Beck has the honor to be entrusted with the SALE of the Entire Valuable Household Furniture etc.etc. at Kempstone Lodge late the Property of Lt. Gen. The Hon. Wm. FitzRoy deceased.

Comprising lofty mahogany four-post bedsteads, with chintz furniture, tent and other bedsteads, superior well-seasoned goose feather beds, bolsters and pillows, Whitney blankets, Marseilles quilts, wool mattresses, mahogany wardrobes and chests of drawers, wash-hand stands and toiletts sets complete, elegant pier and dressing glasses.

Set of handsome mahogany dining tables on pillars and claws, mahogany sofa and other tables, excellant Brussels and Turkey carpets, mahogany sideboards, cellaret and wine coolers, a large quantity of rare old China, consisting of a dinner, dessert, tea and coffee services, cut and plain glass, plated branch and other candlesticks, inkstand etc.etc. about 800 volumes of books, comprising *Hume's History of England* in 13 vols, handsomely bound. *Lord Byron's Works* in 9 volumes, *British Theatre* in 34 volumes, *Addison's Anecdotes* 15 volumes, Walter Scott's *Lady of the Lake*, splendidly bound. *Vancouver's Voyage round the World* 6 Volumes, Hogarth illustrated 3 volumes, 112 Numbers of *Quarterly Reviews* and various other Leading Works. Pair of handsome globes, quite perfect, elegant pedestal and library lamps, single-barrel gun, blunderbuss, brace of excellant pistols, capitol, patent mangle, Large quantity of excellant Kitchen requisites, dairy and brewing utensils etc.etc.

Also a pair of carriage harness, saddles, bridles etc. and every article requisite for the establishment of a Gentleman which he will offer for competition by

Public Auction on Wednesday 25th October and following days Wednesday, Thursday, Friday, Saturday and Monday 25th, 26th, 27th, 28th and 30th days of October and Wednesday 1st November.

The books to be sold the last day.

Appendix 5.

From the Newspapers: An advertisement put in by Mr William Be
Norfolk Chronicle Oct.1837.

Mr William Beck very respectfully calls the Attention of his Agricultural Friends and the Public to the undermentioned valuable Live and Dead Farming Stock late the Property of Lt.General the Hon. William FitzRoy deceased, which he will have the honour to offer for

Sale by Public Auction

on Friday October 13th 1837

comprising

7	very excellant young Cart Horses and Mares
	Riding ditto five years old, quiet to ride and to drive, by Huntingdon.
6	beautiful Ayrshire Cows in full profit
	ditto Heifer forward in Calf
3	yearling Heifers and Steers
	Fine Ayrshire Bull, gentle worker
	Two years old ditto
35	Capitol Store Pigs
27	Weaning ditto
3	good breeding Sows.

The Carriages and Implements

Consist of three excellant waggons, two tumbrels, one small ditto, turnip cart, water cart, corn drill, two iron rools, dressing machine, turnip cutter, mole plough, road ditto, large four-hors ditto complete, two wheat harrows, one pair of five balked ditto, ditto nine-baulker ditto, malt mills, sheep troughs, lifts, hurdles, cross-cut saw, vice, carpenter's bench, cart and plough harness, long and short ladders, fork, ropes, rakes, and various small implements requisite for a large occupation.

The Sale will commence at 11 o'clock precisely, and Refreshments provided previous to the sale of the live Stock.

An important sale of Furniture....every requisite for the establishment of a Gentleman, Public Auction Wednesday 25 October and following Days.

Full particular in future papers.

Appendix 6.

The Will of Lady Elizabeth FitzRoy 1839.

This is the Will of me Lady Elizabeth FitzRoy widow of the late Lt.General William FitzRoy who died on the 19th May 1837 whereas by my Marriage Settlement it is appointed that in case of my having no Children and dyeing intestate the whole of my Paternal Fortune shall revert back to my own Family to be equally divided amongst the surviving Sisters I have thought it just and fair to leave by Will a share of it to each of my Widowed Sisters for their natural Lives and then to go to the benefit of my Husbands Sons and their wives and families after them. Whereas by my marriage settlement I was entitled to dispose of the whole of my paternal Fortune Deed or Will executed in the presence of two witnesses even in the lifetime of my late lamented husband The whole of that paternal Fortune now remains at my disposal and I trust unencumbered. I give and bequeath to my dear Sister Augusta Favel the interest or dividends of four thousand Pounds Stirling part of my paternal Fortune (now charged on the Euston Estate) for her natural life and after her death I give the aforesaid four thousand pounds Stirling to the Rev. Frederick Thomas William Coke FitzRoy my late husband's youngest Son or in the event of his death unto his Widow and Children after her I give to my dear Sister Isabella Blachford the interest or dividends of three thousand pounds part of my paternal Fortune (now charged on George's share of his first wife's a/d marriage settlement and producing an interest of one hundred and twenty pounds per Annum) for my Sister Isabella Blachford's natural Life and after her death I give the aforesaid Sum of three thousand pounds to William Simon Houghton FitzRoy my late husband's oldest Son and in the event of his death to his Widow and Children after her. I give to my dear Sister Frances Churchill three hundred Pounds Stirling I give to my dear Sister Charlotte FitzRoy Fifty Pounds Stirling I give to my brother Lord William FitzRoy Fifty pounds Stirling I give to my brother Lord John FitzRoy Fifty pounds Stirling I give to my nephew FitzRoy Blachford Esq. Fifty pounds Stirling To my Niece Isabella Elizabeth Blachford Fifty pounds Stirling To my Niece Georgiana Anne Sumtha [??]

Fifty Pounds Stirling To my Niece Mrs William Purdon late Augusta Louisa Favel I give Fifty pounds Stirling and to Chamberlain Breeze late Gardiner at Kempstone Lodge I give Fifty pounds Stirling in reward for his long and faithful Services and I also give Fifty pounds Stirling to each of my Executors hereinafter named and appointed and to William Simon Haughton FitzRoy I give and bequeath over and above the reversion of the three thousand pounds before mentioned the sum of one thousand pounds wishing in so doing to fulfil to the letter and promise made to his Father all the Rest and Residue of my Paternal Fortune subject only to the payment of my just debts and my funeral expences (these latter not to exceed one hundred pounds) I give and bequeath to my late husband's third surviving son Charles Henry FitzRoy Lieut. in the Royal Navy being desired that in re-cognicant of his having lost his left arm that she should have the largest share of my Paternal Fortune But in event of his death in my life time I give only four thousand pounds Stirling to his Widow and Children after her and the residue or remainder to William Simon Haughton FitzRoy and to the Rev.Frederick Thomas William Coke FitzRoy (the eldest and youngest Sons of the late Lt. General the Honble. William FitzRoy) to be equally divided between them I appoint Frederick Walpole Keppel Esq. of Lexham Hall Norfolk and George Richards Esq. of Queen Anne Street Marylebone joint Executors of this my Last Will and Testament and hereby revoke all former Wills by me at any time made I declare this my Last Will and Testament xxxxxxxx In Witness whereof I hereunto have subscribed and set my Seal this second day of August one thousand eight hundred and thirty eight Elizabeth FitzRoy

Witnesses: James Hoste Clk.
            Robert Sewell Professor of Music Norwich

Proved at London 22 June 1839.

Appendix 7.

In 1851, during the time of the 2nd Earl of Leicester, his agent Mr Keary made a report of all the farms on the Holkham Estate.

Kempstone Lodge Farm in the Parishes of Kempstone and Beeston occupied by Mr W. M. Farrer, contains 438 acres Or Op. Rent £630.00.00. Shooting £15.00.00.
Average Rent per Acre £01.09.05.

Bounded north by Litcham Common, west by Dunham and East Lexham, south by Mr Chamberlaine's Farm (Manor Farm) and Large's Estate and on the East by a rivulet which separates Kempstone from Beeston parish.

The House and premises are surrounded by about 70 acres of Grass land, the greater part of which is very good and may be improved by draining.

To the south of this is Hall close, a fine brown loam upon clay, a very rich and excellent field, it adjoins the southern boundary and is detached from the other ploughed fields by the pastures, crossing which are some very useful arable fields, varying somewhat in depth of soil, but good corn lands; east of these and adjoining the rivulet is a long strip of water meadows which extends to Litcham common. The southern end of it is by far the best and produces an immense quantity of early feeds, the northern and lighter is only made productive by the artificial means of water, as its soil is light and poor and would otherwise produce but little herbage; it is however on the whole a very valuable field supplying early feed for sheep in spring and a heavy crop of excellent hay afterwards.

West of these fields the arable land now extends to the East Lexham boundary, varying a good deal in staple and quality, the north side of each, as they approach the common being light and sandy, while the upper and southern portions, resting upon clay, are better and more tenacious, they have however all of them a bleak northern aspect.

After crossing the road from Swaffham to Litcham there are two or three fields which are very light, poor and unproductive, especially

Kempstone bottom, a piece of rough pasture covered with furze, extremely wet and of little or no value in its present state, requiring very much to be drained and improved. High Field adjoining it is very light and sandy where it skirts the cover, but improves very much on the southwest where it joins Mr Chamberlaine's farm.

General Remarks

Kempstone Lodge Farm is well laid out with convenient roads and straight fences, most of the internal ones are good and have been well attended to, they abound however in immense quantities, with young trees, which are injurious alike to them and the crops: the outer or boundary fences are mostly bad and in an unsatisfactory state, and they do not present any features of improvement. [1]

The Premises are not well placed for the occupation of some of the ploughed land, and 80 acres of the poorest of it are at some distance. The Tenant has erected a new bullock yard and shed in Kempstone bottom, for the convenience of making manure in that portion of the farm thus saving cartage both of roots and manure, it is not however in the very best place and if a more permanent building were erected a better site should certainly be chosen.

The grass lands have evidently suffered much from want of drainage and several of the ploughed fields said to be drained, require doing again more effectually. The Pastures near the House and the water meadows, are capable of being made most productive for surpassing in quality the generality of grass lands in Norfolk. The light arable soils would doubtless be benefited by a moderate use of clay, which abounds on the western side of the farm and a higher system of farming than that hitherto pursued will unquestionably increase the produce of a soil which appears somewhat cold and sterile unless highly farmed.

The House which combines every requisite for a gentleman's residence, consists of a small Hall, dining room, drawing room and anti-room, breakfast room and study; excellent Kitchen and housekeeper's room, Servants Hall etc five or six good bedrooms, dressing rooms and ample servants apartments, all upon the second floor, there being no attic.

It is built of white bricks and covered with blue pantiles and is in substantial repair, some portion of the roof admits the rain but it is thought nothing more than a few cracked or broken tiles is the cause, it is however an extremely damp house which might be in some measure remidied [sic] by a deep drain around it.

The Farm premises which are placed at a convenient distance from the house consist of a very large and roomy barn, carthouse stable for 14 horses, two bullock yards capable of holding 30 oxen and several loose boxes, cowyard and enclosed shed, two horse yards and shed, small colts yard and shed, hayhouse, piggeries, Cakehouse, carpenter's shop and Waggon lodge with granary over. These premises are by no means well-arranged and some parts over done and superfluous while others are deficient.

They are all built of stones and bricks and covered with pan tiles: the timbers in most of the roofs are tolerably good but as the tiles will one day require to be replaced with a more durable material such as slate, it is probable some of them may require attention.

The Bailiff's house which stands in the yard is now divided into two dwellings and contains two sitting rooms and four bedrooms, it is built of stones and covered with blue pan tiles.

There are four more cottages let with this Farm, three of which are in a pasture at the extreme Southwest corner of it, they are built of bricks and covered with pan tiles which are by no means in very good order. Each contains a sitting room, small leanto pantry, and two bedrooms, and if in good repair they would be comfortable cottages.

The last which forms a sort of lodge to the entrance from Litcham common is a low and small thatched building, containing only two rooms on the ground floor, it is however in very tolerable repair.

May 1851.

[1] by fences he means hedges.